ASTROLOGY
Your Wheel of Fortune

*the text of this book is printed
on 100% recycled paper*

ASTROLOGY
Your Wheel of Fortune

NORVELL

BARNES & NOBLE BOOKS
A DIVISION OF HARPER & ROW, PUBLISHERS
New York, Hagerstown, San Francisco, London

ASTROLOGY: YOUR WHEEL OF FORTUNE. Copyright © 1975 by Anthony Norvell. All rights reserved. Printed in the United States of America. No part of this book may be used or reproduced in any manner without written permission except in the case of brief quotations embodied in critical articles and reviews. For information address Harper & Row, Publishers, Inc., 10 East 53d Street, New York, N.Y. 10022. Published simultaneously in Canada by Fitzhenry & Whiteside Limited, Toronto.

First BARNES & NOBLE BOOKS edition published 1974.

LIBRARY OF CONGRESS CATALOG CARD NUMBER: 74-9258

STANDARD BOOK NUMBER: 06-464008-6

76 77 10 9 8 7 6 5 4 3

Contents

	Introduction	1
1	The Twelve Signs of the Zodiac: Know Your True Character	6
2	What Profession Should You Choose According to Astrology?	21
3	Your Star Guide to Happiness in Love and Marriage	37
4	How the Stars Affect Your Children and Their Destinies	50
5	How to Use Astrology to Become Successful and Rich	66
6	How to Use Astrology to Make You a Social Success	95
7	How Your Stars Affect Your Health and Length of Life	105
8	For Women Only: Things You Should Know About Male Friends, Husbands, and Lovers	114
9	For Men Only: Things You Should Know About Female Friends, Sweethearts, and Wives	123
10	How Your Stars Can Bring You Peace of Mind, Joy, and Fulfillment	133
11	How Your Stars Can Help You Develop Artistic and Creative Talents	143
12	Your Ultimate Destiny According to Your Birthsign	154

Introduction

In recent years scientists have been studying the effects of sunspots and the magnetic and electrical currents that bombard our earth from outer space, affecting radio and television transmission and reception. They discovered something the ancients knew centuries ago: that man *is* affected by the planets and their action in our solar system. This ancient science was named astrology.

During recent years of scientific observation of sunspot cycles and radioactivity from the planets, it was found that during the height of sunspot activity there were more suicides than under normal solar activity. It was also discovered that sporadic wars broke out all over the world, that there were more crimes of violence, more divorces, and more revolutions and social unrest than during normal solar activity.

This discovery that the planets do affect humans has led to a re-evaluation of the ancient studies by the Egyptian, Babylonian, and Assyrian astrologers, who claimed that the moment a person was born he was imprinted with a solar programming that affected his character and his destiny.

As destiny is the outer result of a person's character, it is obvious that understanding his character according to the solar influences at the time of his birth can help man profoundly alter his birth-path and achieve a fortunate destiny.

In this book we shall study only the influence of the sun on one's life and destiny. All the planets in our solar system are said to have an effect on a person's life, but as the sun is the strongest and most important body in our solar system, we are concerned with its effect on destiny.

Each sign of the zodiac is said to have a ruling planet. The planets are the sun, moon, Mercury, Venus, Mars, Jupiter, Saturn, Uranus, and Neptune. They rule the following twelve signs of the zodiac.

The sun rules Leo, called a fire sign.
The moon rules Cancer, known as a water sign.
Mercury rules the signs of Gemini, an air sign, and Virgo, an earth sign.
Venus rules the signs of Taurus, an earth sign, and Libra, an air sign.
Mars rules the fire sign Aries, and also the water sign Scorpio.
Jupiter is the ruler of the fire sign Sagittarius.
Saturn rules over the earth sign of Capricorn.
Uranus is the ruler of the air sign Aquarius.
Neptune rules the water sign of Pisces.

The position of the sun in the zodiac at the time of your birth determines the vital energy released by that planet and affects the cells of your brain and body. The angle of the rays hitting the earth affects a person differently in the spring when the rays are not as strong as in the summer. The sun's rays affect you with their magnetism, electricity, and radioactive waves. They motivate you to be the type of person you are, shape your character, and push you in the direction of the life experiences that will be fortunate or unfortunate.

It is the sun's position in your chart at the time of birth that gives you the drive and energy to fulfill your life goal.

If you were born when the solar rays were weak you may find life more difficult. The challenges of life may get you down and make you feel that you were born under an "unlucky" star.

Some people seem to have a brilliant destiny without making much effort. Everything good seems to come to them. They go into the right work and are a big success; they find love and marry the perfect mate; and they seem to live charmed lives. We say of such people, "They were born under a lucky star."

In a sense this is true, for the wheel of fortune is fixed at the time of birth by the position of the sun and the other planets. The sun, being the most powerful, exerts the greatest influence and that is why it is vitally important to know in what sign of the zodiac you were born and how this will affect your destiny.

The sun is the determining factor in shaping character and inclining one towards a certain type of destiny. The wheel of fortune inclines you to be the type of person you are; it gives you certain characteristics; it programs your mind with electromagnetic wavelengths that trigger certain actions in your life.

The other planets' influences can be determined only by setting up a complete horoscope of the time, place, month, date, and year of a person's birth. The solar influence is only one facet of the personal horoscope; however, the importance of the sun in our planetary system is the determining factor that makes you an Aries, a Scorpio, or a Piscean.

All people born in the same sign are *not* alike, but they do possess similar characteristics which incline them to act in a similar way. That is why, once you know a person's sun sign, you have a key to his character and can accurately judge what his actions will be in any given situation.

However, astrology is not the sole determining influence in a person's destiny. There are three other factors: heredity, education, and environment. These mitigate the stars' influences and often alter the destiny.

A Lincoln, born in the sign of genius, Aquarius, can have a solar twin, born on the same date and the same place, who might turn out to be a complete failure or even a criminal. This does *not* mean that the stars did not give him the same traits and potentials as a Lincoln, but that the failure chose to exercise his power of will or choice to go in a different direction. He was also affected by his education, his environment, and the hereditary pattern of his parents' genes.

Astrology must be thought of as a guidepost to the future. By knowing your tendencies and character better, you can begin to work intelligently to overcome your weaknesses and strengthen your good points. You can be inspired to a more successful life by studying the lives of great men and women born under your sign. You can also learn of their mistakes and how you may avoid them, so that you can achieve your full star-given potentials for greatness.

There are sections in this book that deal with character, business, money, romance, marriage, children, health, happiness, and ultimate goal fulfillment. You can be guided to the choice of the right occupation; you can learn the most compatible signs for you in love and marriage; you will be told some of the pitfalls that afflict your sign and how to take steps to avoid them.

There is a saying in astrology, "The stars impel, they do not compel." You need not come into the disasters and problems that your stars might incline you to if you study your sign of the zodiac and learn your good and bad points. Then you can more intelligently meet the challenges of life and turn them into stepping-stones to future success.

A physicist of the United States Weather Bureau wrote recently that our earth exists in time and space, surrounded by electrical and magnetic fields that affect the earth. There are alpha particles and electrons that the sun shoots out into space, and possibly even the stars themselves have such radiations that can affect our earth. There are also cosmic rays and other wavelengths that come to earth from outer space, affecting our earth and certainly motivating people.

In this mysterious universe the ancients knew that the stars in the heavens, particularly the sun, bombarded the earth with magnetism and forces of energy that had a drastic effect on all living things. It is this solar activity that we are concerned with in a study of astrology.

Every sign of the zodiac can be good or bad, depending on your use of the qualities you were given by your stars. A shrewd, highly gifted person, born under the best influences, may pervert that solar energy and suffer the consequences. A former head of the New York Stock Exchange who once made millions of dollars could have been said to be born under a lucky star. However, he was convicted of fraud and sent to prison for several years. He could have shaped his destiny in the direction of honesty and achieved success if he had avoided the destructive actions which led to his downfall.

Learn how to make the most of your good qualities by knowing the tendencies of your solar sign in the zodiac. If there are unfortunate planetary influences in your chart, work harder, become better educated, change your environment, take advantage of all the social assistance available to direct your energies towards greater success and personal fulfillment of the great destiny that can be yours, no matter in which sign of the zodiac you were born.

Find out your correct sign according to this table.

THE TWELVE SIGNS OF THE ZODIAC

Aries	March 21 to April 20
Taurus	April 21 to May 20
Gemini	May 21 to June 20
Cancer	June 21 to July 22
Leo	July 23 to Aug. 22
Virgo	Aug. 23 to Sept. 22
Libra	Sept. 23 to Oct. 22
Scorpio	Oct. 23 to Nov. 22
Sagittarius	Nov. 23 to Dec. 21
Capricorn	Dec. 22 to Jan. 19
Aquarius	Jan. 20 to Feb. 18
Pisces	Feb. 19 to March 20

If you were born between the 20th and 23d of any month, you are said to be born on the cusp of two signs. You then partake of the characteristics of each sign and you would have to look up your date of birth in an ephemeris to determine the exact position of the sun. The sun changes positions in relation to the earth approximately between the 20th and the 23d of each month.

1

The Twelve Signs of the Zodiac: Know Your True Character

Astrology can reveal your true character and show you how to achieve your ultimate destiny. Through character you act out a part on the stage of life. If you assume the character of a villain, no matter what sign you were born under, you can be sure that your life will reflect tragedy and disaster. If you choose the role of a hero, then even if you were born under a so-called weak planet your life can become prosperous, romantic, and rewarding.

Goethe said:

> Sow a thought, reap a habit;
> Sow a habit, reap a character;
> Sow a character, reap a destiny.

When you know your true character, according to the sign under which you were born, you may play the role you choose more realistically in your life drama. All signs have potentials of greatness, and all signs possess weaknesses which can lead one to destruction and failure. By knowing the traits and tendencies for your sign you can implement the strong points of your character and lessen the weaknesses.

IF YOU WERE BORN IN ARIES
March 21 to April 20

Aries is the first sign in the zodiac and is said to be one of the strongest. This sign gives qualities of leadership, courage, and greatness. If you work to strengthen these natural qualities you can rise to a position of power and greatness.

But if you choose to subvert these natural qualities of your sign it can lead to disaster and defeat. Hitler was born in Aries, and had he chosen to be a hero, he might have led the German people to greatness. Instead he chose to play the role of villain and emphasized the qualities of stubbornness, cruelty, and aggression, which are the negative characteristics often exhibited by those born in Aries.

Mars, the ruling planet of this sign, is the planet of war, but also rules surgeons, generals, and leaders. Some of the world's greatest people, Thomas Jefferson, for example, were born in Aries.

If you were born in the sign of Aries, you are a natural-born leader. You will blaze your way to the top in whatever field you choose. This means that you possess tremendous vitality and energy. You absorbed the dynamic qualities of the fiery planet Mars when you were born and inhaled your first breath.

The ancients gave this sign the symbol of the ram, because Aries people are so determined they often butt their way out of difficulties and stubbornly adhere to a chosen course of action. Sometimes these traits of determination and aggression can deteriorate into stubbornness, willfulness, and obstinacy. Very often Arians start with a burst of energy to rise to the top in their chosen field, then become restless or bored and change their plans in mid-course. This tendency often leads to their failure and untimely defeat.

Aries is probably one of the most talented of all signs in the zodiac. As this sign rules the head and brains, Arians are often highly intellectual and take to a college education. Many of those born in Aries become successful in industry, politics, writing, music, acting, and directing.

Some of Hollywood's first stars who were leaders in the motion picture industry were Arians, among them Gloria Swanson, Mary Pickford, Charlie Chaplin, and Harold Lloyd. In more recent times such stars as Marlon Brando, Debbie Reynolds, Doris Day, and William Holden were born in this sign.

Others who achieved greatness and who were born in Aries were Presidents John Tyler and Thomas Jefferson, Henry Clay, William Wordsworth, Washington Irving, and businessmen J. Pierpont Morgan and Charles Schwab.

If you are born in the fortunate sign of Aries you will find yourself energetic, active, and ambitious. You are eager to rise to the top in whatever field you choose to express your talents. Your weakness is that you may undertake too many things at the same time and quickly lose interest. You have a knack for starting things but never finishing them, and you must cultivate qualities of persistence and patience.

You make friends easily but your Mars temper is apt to cause you to lose them quickly. You must curb your temper, control your enthusiasm, and conserve your energies for the long haul rather than the quick, easy goal that might not last.

In other chapters dealing with professions, business matters, money, investments, love, and marriage, you will learn of the tendencies in these various areas of your life, and you will learn how you can create a star-given destiny of happiness, health, love-fulfillment, and success.

IF YOU WERE BORN IN TAURUS
April 21 to May 20

Taurus is the second sign of the zodiac and is ruled by Venus, the planet of beauty and love. It is considered one of the most creative and artistic signs. Many actors, singers, artists, and authors were born in Taurus. However, Taurus is said to rule the second house in the natural zodiac, and this often makes Taureans big money-makers and good businessmen.

As this sign rules the throat area, many singers were born under it. The following singers and actors are Taureans: Bing Crosby, Dean Martin, Pat Boone, Kate Smith, Shirley Temple, Carol Burnett. You will note that these Taurus-born are all gifted performers, renowned for their vocal abilities. Also, some of the past great movie stars were born in this sign, including Gary Cooper, Tyrone Power, Alice Faye, and Margaret Sullavan.

If you were born in this gifted sign you will have much self-reliance and ambition to succeed. You do not love money, but you *like* the things money can do and as you appreciate an environment of comfort, even luxury, you strive hard to achieve a high goal that will give you material success.

Your ruling planet Venus gives you a strong love nature. You are sympathetic, kind, and very generous. You enjoy a beautiful home where you can have the things you love around you. You enjoy beautiful music, good books, fine food, and pleasant companions.

Venus emphasizes your social side. You are generally well-liked and are inclined to hold your friends and stick by them through thick and thin.

Check the lives of the following Taureans and you will be helped to better understand your own vast potential for fame and greatness: Presidents James Buchanan, James Monroe, U. S. Grant, and Harry Truman; Shakespeare, Marie Corelli, Herbert Spencer, and Dante; the Duke of Wellington, explorer Robert Peary, and publisher William Randolph Hearst.

IF YOU WERE BORN IN GEMINI
May 21 to June 20

Gemini is the third sign of the zodiac. Its symbol is the twins, and it is typical of Geminis to be dual in nature. At times they can be the most charming, brilliant, and witty people. At other times they can be very reserved, serious, and moody. Mercury, the ruling planet of this sign, is said to rule the mental and intellectual faculties.

If you are Gemini-born you should strive to get the best education possible. The brilliant mind you possess is enhanced by wisdom and knowledge. You can rise to the top in your chosen profession. The Gemini women make good teachers and instructors. The men are excellent lawyers and businessmen. They often go into politics with great success. John F. Kennedy was a typical Gemini, with his wit, charm, and culture, and also his ability to persuade people to do his bidding. Hubert H. Humphrey was also born in Gemini, as was the Duchess of Windsor, who charmed a king off his throne.

If you were born in this talented sign, the best thing about your character is that you are versatile, adaptable, charming, and diplomatic. You have the art of winning friends and holding them.

You enjoy the company of people and like to entertain your close friends and see them enjoying themselves. Geminis are great wits and are noted for their sense of humor and ability to make people laugh. Bob Hope is typically Gemini; in his public personality he is a great clown, but in his personal life he has the typical Gemini duality and is serious, deeply emotional, and sympathetic. His tendency to do charitable acts for others is also typical of the Gemini character.

Just as there is a good side to Gemini so, too, there is a negative side. The planet Mercury often makes Geminis moody, nervous, and irritable. They are often hard to understand and must have sympathy and love constantly. They are impatient with others and often fret and fume when people keep them waiting or show other signs of human weakness.

Because Gemini is such a talented sign, people born under it can succeed in any occupation where they use the higher creative intelligence they possess. Having so many possibilities, they often scatter their energies in many directions until they reach the age of twenty-five or thirty. This often delays their success in life, and they come into full stride in their forties.

The Gemini-born can adapt to many different occupations, but the planet Mercury makes them most successful in occupations dealing with the creative mind and intellect. They are excellent in writing, journalism, television reporting, teaching, languages, publicity, advertising, interior decorating, as well as promoting those who are artists, writers, actors, singers, and inventors. They are especially good in the publishing field as writers, editors, or publishers. They make good TV directors, producers, or actors.

Among the famous people born in Gemini are Ralph Waldo Emerson, Walt Whitman, Sir Arthur Conan Doyle, Patrick Henry, Jefferson Davis, Nathan Hale, Nathaniel Greene, Richard Wagner, Rembrandt, Pope Pius X, Brigham Young, and William Rockefeller.

IF YOU WERE BORN IN CANCER
June 21 to July 22

The sign of Cancer is the fourth sign of the zodiac. Its ruling planet is the moon, and its symbol is the crab. Like the crab, most people born in Cancer progress slowly by seemingly taking two steps sidewise and one step forward. Caution is the keyword of this sign. You are reserved, reflective, and unusually cautious. You generally make progress in life through great prudence and economy. This is often called the money sign, for it gives those born in it the ability to sense public needs and fill them. It is a highly intuitive sign.

You have been given great ability for business and have a very practical and tactful nature. You can achieve success through your ability to adapt to changing conditions, to anticipate the needs of others, and to handle all matters connected with finances, houses, land, and other material possessions.

Your nature is domestic and sentimental. You enjoy the home and are a natural family lover, making an excellent parent.

Cancer rules the early life, the home environment, parents, and the end of life. Relatives mean a good deal to the typical Cancerian, and he likes to surround himself with those close to him and lives for family connections. Many Cancer people come into their greatest success late in life, and they often live to a ripe old age. The first John D. Rockefeller was born in Cancer. Not only did he attain great wealth, founding the Rockefeller fortune, but he lived to be nearly a hundred years of age. His son John D. Rockefeller, Jr., was also a Cancerian.

Famous people born in the sign of Cancer include Presidents John Quincy Adams and Calvin Coolidge; Rubens, the great artist; Nathaniel Hawthorne and Jean Jacques Rousseau, authors; businessmen Stuyvesant Fish and John Wanamaker; the Duke of Windsor; actress Barbara Stanwyck; and actor James Cagney.

IF YOU WERE BORN IN LEO
July 23 to Aug. 22

Leo is considered the "royal" sign in the zodiac, as people born in this sign often seem to have extraordinary good luck and to lead charmed lives. It has also been noted that more members of royalty were born in the sign of Leo than any other sign, including Caesar, Napoleon, and Alexander the Great.

Leo rules over the entertainment world, and many outstanding figures in music, literature, the theater, screen, and television were born in this sign.

If you are Leo-born, your ruling planet is the sun and the symbol for your sign is the lion. It is interesting to note that at one time the powerful motion-picture studio Metro-Goldwyn-Mayer had as its trademark a lion. When I was known as an advisor to the movie stars, I checked on the stars at that studio and found that the principal MGM stars were born in Leo. These were Myrna Loy, William Powell, Robert Taylor, and Norma Shearer, who were at that time among the biggest money-makers in the industry.

This sign makes you very aggressive, dominant, and courageous.

You are inclined to rise to high levels of achievement because of these traits, and you never stop trying until you achieve your life goal.

You have great executive ability and make a good manager or head of a business. You are ambitious and determined, and when in the wrong work or position you become highly nervous and frustrated, seeking always a position of power and leadership.

The Leo-born are often called self-centered, but I find that most of them want money and power so that they can share their good with others. You are extremely generous and magnanimous. There is nothing small or petty about your mind. You can rise to high levels socially, and people gravitate to your center of magnetism. Born when the sun is high in the heavens in midsummer, you seem to attract people of every type to your magic circle of charm and magnetism.

Among the famous people born in the sign of Leo are Herbert Hoover, Queen Mother Elizabeth of England, Benito Mussolini, George Bernard Shaw, Booth Tarkington, Edna Ferber, Jacqueline Kennedy Onassis, Henry Ford, General Hugh Johnson, and Bernard Baruch.

IF YOU WERE BORN IN VIRGO
Aug. 23 to Sept. 22

This sign of the zodiac is ruled by the planet Mercury which governs the mind and intellect. It also controls the nervous system. You have a very rapid mind, a good memory, and a very practical nature. Virgo is called the earth sign and it often makes you very serious, contemplative, and reserved.

You are a strange combination of the practical and the daydreamer. You like things connected with business, but you are also artistic and creative, loving art, music, books, and things of beauty. You value your privacy and resent people intruding in your environment, although you can be very sociable when you want to be. People are apt to think you rather cold and unemotional at times, but this is owing to your reserve and your tendency to put everything through the logical, reasoning brain that directs you in every department of your life.

There is a tendency to vacillation and change, and this must be watched so that you do not give in to indecision and make errors in judgment which might exact a price.

Virgo people are very good in any work that requires tact and diplomacy. They are good in dealing with the public and make excellent salesmen. The women are good teachers and often rise to supervisory positions owing to their thoroughness and efficiency. Virgos make good writers and critics. They often become musically involved as they have precision and rhythm. They are very adaptable, as their mercurial dispositions tend to love of change and travel, and they can fit with ease into any situation.

The following famous people were born in the sign of Virgo: Presidents William H. Taft and Lyndon B. Johnson; writers O. Henry, Leo Tolstoi, Oliver Wendell Holmes, Bret Harte, Upton Sinclair, and H. G. Wells. Margaret Sanger, the pioneer advocate of birth control, was a Virgo, as were also the Marquis de Lafayette and Cardinal Richelieu. In the motion picture world Greta Garbo, Ingrid Bergman, Peter Sellers, Claudette Colbert, and Frederic March were born in Virgo, as was Gaylord Hauser, the noted writer on health and diet.

IF YOU WERE BORN IN LIBRA
Sept. 23 to Oct. 22

This sign of the zodiac is ruled by the planet of peace, beauty, and love, Venus. It makes the Libra-born kind, gentle, and loving. They hate discord and confusion in their environment and thrive best in an atmosphere of sociability, romance, and beauty.

Libra people are idealistic and romantic. They are in love with love, and very often they misjudge the person they think they love and wake up to find that this person was not suited to them.

Your nature is kind and generous, and you take great pride in keeping your environment peaceful and beautiful. You love a home and family and usually marry early in life and start your own family.

As the scales are the symbol of your sign, it is vitally important that you strive to maintain mental and emotional balance at all times. You are apt to be high-strung and very sensitive to your environment. You attract people because of your charm and affability, but you have to guard constantly against being betrayed by those who might take advantage of your good nature.

Your highly sensitive nature makes you respond to beauty in all forms. You often study art and you may become interested in music as a hobby; you could take to writing poetry or romantic stories and achieve some success in that field.

You love to travel and move about frequently, as you have great curiosity to see the world. You may at some time in your life interest yourself in social betterment. Some of the world's great reformers and leaders were born in Libra, including Eleanor Roosevelt, who constantly worked to help the unfortunate, and Gandhi of India who gave his life for the liberation of his countrymen.

Others born in this sign of the zodiac were Presidents Chester A. Arthur, Zachary Taylor, and Rutherford B. Hayes. Annie Besant, the founder of theosophy, was a Libra, as were also Nietzsche, Admiral Lord Nelson, Franz Liszt, Max Schmeling, Eleanora Duse, Sarah Bernhardt, Helen Hayes, Greer Garson, Melina Mercouri, and June Allyson. General Eisenhower was an outstanding example of the typical Libra-born.

IF YOU WERE BORN IN SCORPIO
Oct. 23 to Nov. 22

Scorpio is one of the strongest and most vital signs of the zodiac. Your ruling planet Mars is known for its fiery and impetuous qualities.

As a Scorpio you will have a very strong will and you must be very positive, determined, and even obstinate. You strive to rise to very high goals, and at times you might have to climb over others to get there. Sometimes Scorpios can be ruthless and make very bitter enemies, but most of them are inclined to be loyal. They make excellent friends and loyal mates.

Robert Kennedy, a typical Scorpio, showed much concern for the welfare of deprived people. His death by assassination was clearly shown in his chart, for the eighth house, which Scorpio rules, had two planets afflicted, Saturn and Mars, causing death by firearms and violence.

The Mars-born must control the temper and the tongue. If you are Scorpio you are apt to have a sarcastic wit, and other people may feel that you are being deliberately cruel and cutting in your thoughtless remarks.

Scorpio people are especially determined to achieve a goal of fame and fortune. They never like to be in inferior positions in life, and they usually become rich through their creative ideas. Scorpios respect money and the things money can do. They are usually very generous with members of their family and with close friends, but they can also be very frugal and thrifty in order to accumulate a fortune. Hetty Green, the famous woman who built a fortune of one hundred million dollars through skillful stock-market manipulation, was a Scorpio. She was called a miser, but she achieved her objective in life, which was to accumulate a huge fortune and have security for the future.

Other famous people born in Scorpio were actor Richard Burton; Spiro Agnew, who became vice-president, only to resign under fire; King Edward VII and Voltaire; Presidents James Garfield (who was assassinated), Warren G. Harding, James Polk, and Theodore Roosevelt; authors Robert Louis Stevenson and Macaulay; Cheiro, the famous Count Hamon of London, who was one of the world's greatest palm readers; Martin Luther; Samuel Insull; Madame Marie Curie; and Ignace Paderewski. Also born in this famous sign were actors Will Rogers, Marie Dressler, Jackie Coogan, Hedy Lamarr, Dick Powell, Eleanor Powell, and Vivien Leigh of *Gone With the Wind* fame.

IF YOU WERE BORN IN SAGITTARIUS
Nov. 23 to Dec. 21

The fire sign of Sagittarius is ruled by the beneficent planet Jupiter. This is considered one of the best signs of the zodiac and bestows upon you a kind, benevolent, and honest character. You were born to rule and govern others. Many people born in this excellent sign become government leaders and politicians, and they are just, honorable, and honest.

The symbol of this fire sign is that of the archer, showing a creature that is half man and half horse aiming his arrows into the sky. The typical Sagittarius-born is of the earth, but his mind and his thoughts are in the sky. He aims towards lofty goals. He is idealistic and lofty in his concepts and actions.

This sign, which rules the ninth house in the zodiac, is said to govern matters connected with religious thought, philosophy, and travel. If you are typical of this sign you will be a deep thinker, affectionate, loyal, and ardent. You may be moody at times and easily hurt because you are very sensitive. You must strive to understand the motives of others and forgive them for what may seem to be cruelty but is in fact only thoughtlessness.

The keyword that best designates the character of the typical Sagittarian is independence. You like to be free and to act independently of others. This means that you should strive to get into a position that does not require you to punch a time clock or be under constant supervision. You are best suited to work where you can be your own boss. A business of your own would be the ideal situation for you.

Because of your love of freedom of action, it is very wise to avoid any marriage with a mate who is jealous or overly possessive. Many Sagittarians prefer to remain free rather than risk their happiness in marriage. However, if you learn to curb your sense of independence to some extent, there is no reason why marriage should not bring you happiness and fulfillment.

Many famous people were born in this lucky sign, including King George VI, the Duke of Kent, Benjamin Disraeli, President Martin Van Buren; authors Mark Twain, John Greenleaf Whittier, John Milton, Noel Coward, Arthur Brisbane, and Erskine Caldwell; composer Ludwig van Beethoven; philanthropist Andrew Carnegie; Joe DiMaggio; James H. Doolittle; oil billionaire J. Paul Getty; John V. Lindsay; Adam Clayton Powell; Margaret Chase Smith; and Strom Thurmond.

IF YOU WERE BORN IN CAPRICORN
Dec. 22 to Jan. 19

You were born in the winter months when the sun's rays are not as strong as in spring or summer, but what you lack in fire, passion, and inspiration, you make up for in durability, persistence, and determination. You seldom achieve your high goals easily or quickly, for your ruling planet Saturn seems intent on testing you by fire to prove your worth. But Capricorns do eventually achieve their goals, for the symbol of this determined sign is the goat, and this sure-footed creature tests every rock on its perilous journey to the mountaintop.

If you were born in this rugged sign, you may have many tough battles ahead of you, but by cultivating quiet determination and maintaining your inner poise, you will override all negative forces and grow stronger as you grow older.

Many Capricorn people enjoy being in positions of power. They like to rule rather than be ruled. They are successful because they can be very single-minded and they never let anything or anyone deflect them from their goal. They are leaders and doers of the zodiac and they seldom follow the pack.

Some of the world's most famous people were born in the sign of Capricorn, including Sir Isaac Newton, Benjamin Franklin, Joseph Stalin, John Hancock, and Daniel Webster; Presidents Andrew Johnson, Millard Fillmore, and Woodrow Wilson; authors Rudyard Kipling, Louis Bromfield, Jack London, Edgar Allan Poe, and Alexander Woollcott. Also, in our own time, are J. Edgar Hoover, Howard Hughes, James Baldwin, Mrs. Lyndon B. Johnson, and Elvis Presley.

IF YOU WERE BORN IN AQUARIUS
Jan. 20 to Feb. 18

You were born in the sign that has more people in the Hall of Fame than any other sign in the zodiac. You have a right to be proud if you are an Aquarian, for it seems that the stars have endowed this superior sign with more high qualities and virtues than any other sign.

You were endowed with a brilliant mind; in fact, you could pass as a genius. You are way in advance of most people in your intellectual capacity to grasp any subject and to act intuitively in any given crisis. A typical Aquarian was the late Franklin Delano Roosevelt, the only man ever to be elected four times to the office of president of the United States. His charm, wit, magnetism, and powers of persuasion were such that millions of people came under his sway. But he was also hated and had his periods of misfortune, including a bout with polio that left him crippled for life.

Most Aquarians rise high in life but they are always threatened with some calamity. Edison was one and he became deaf. Kaiser

Wilhelm was an emperor one day and wound up being a woodchopper the next. Lord Byron had a club foot. Charles Lindbergh, after winning plaudits of the world for his daring feat in crossing the ocean in a single-seated plane, had sudden tragedy strike him when his infant son was kidnapped and killed. Abraham Lincoln, perhaps the most famous of all Aquarians, was assassinated.

So, too, if you are an Aquarian you can rise to great heights, but you must constantly beware of disasters and defeats, for the brighter the light, the darker the shadow it casts. You can overcome this tendency by being aware of your own potential and then striving to act within its boundaries, not striving to sail too high without preparing a suitable foundation for your future fame and glory.

You possess a high degree of intuition and may become interested in mysticism, astrology, and philosophy. The noted astrologer Evangeline Adams was born in Aquarius.

We are said to be in the Aquarian age, as this sign, ruled by the strange and mysterious planet Uranus, represents all that is advanced and modern, including aviation and space travel, electronics, television, the automotive industry, computer machines, and other modern advances in technology, science, and industry.

Fame can come easily to you if you were born in this lucky sign, but you have to be extremely careful not to let yourself be deflected from your goal by emotional turbulence, chaos and confusion, and misdirected passions in the department of love and marriage. Many Aquarians marry more than once, and they often have tremendous problems in love and marriage. You are inclined to be intolerant, impatient of others' shortcomings, and desirous of ruling and dominating outer events and other people. You are a better boss than worker and are at home in any field where you can use science or modern methods to help you achieve your goal in life. You are a dreamer and have tremendous imagination and vision. You can set lofty goals for yourself and for others to follow. You will leave your footsteps on the sands of time in some unique way that makes people remember you.

The following famous people were born in the sign of Aquarius: William McKinley, Aaron Burr, Robert Burns, Charles Lamb, Jules Verne, Charles Dickens, Charles Darwin, Galileo, Swedenborg, Dwight L. Moody, Mozart, Sir Henry Irving, Adelina Patti, John Barrymore, Clark Gable, noted jockey Eddie Arcaro,

General Omar Bradley, Norman Mailer, James Michener, Ronald Reagan, Jackie Robinson, Norman Rockwell, Dean Rusk, Mrs. Harry Truman, Margaret Truman, and Jersey Joe Walcott.

IF YOU WERE BORN IN PISCES
Feb. 19 to March 20

Neptune is the ruling planet of this fascinating and mysterious sign. There is a strange duality about the typical Pisces person. In fact, the ancients symbolized this sign with two fish, one swimming upstream, the other downstream. So, too, Pisceans are apt to feel this duality in their nature. One side wants to soar into unattainable realms of dreams and fantasies; the other is very much concerned with such mundane matters as earning money and achieving security in life. The Piscean dreads poverty and being dependent on someone else for support in old age.

As this sign rules the twelfth house in the zodiac, called the house of self-undoing, you must be very careful not to make mistakes arising from your own vacillation, indecision, and wavering nature. There is likely to be some emotional turbulence, and the emotions, rather than the head, are apt to rule you. This often leads to self-indulgence, the forming of negative habits that can include laziness, drinking or smoking excessively, or gambling. A strong Piscean avoids these pitfalls, knowing that they can lead to complications, danger, and even financial ruin.

Another thing that you must beware of, if born in this easygoing, genial, and friendly sign, is that other people are likely to take advantage of your good nature. They may borrow money from you and never repay it, and when you demand payment of the loan, they are apt to become enemies. You must guard against becoming involved in in-law problems that can lead to disaster in marriage.

You are the type that people always turn to in misfortune, and your sympathetic nature makes you tolerant and helpful. In fact, Pisceans are the natural do-gooders of the world, trying to help the unfortunate, elevate the fallen, and encourage the weak and indigent. Often you may become involved in the worries and problems of others to your own personal neglect.

But if these are Piscean weaknesses, there are also certain

strengths and positive qualities of this sign which help you overcome many of the misfortunes of this sign.

Pisces is said to be one of the highest developed of all signs of the zodiac in a spiritual sense. It was called the twelfth house of karma by the ancients who believed that when they were born in this lofty, idealistic, self-sacrificing sign of the zodiac they had paid all their karmic debts in life and were ready for life's greatest spiritual rewards. It is found that Pisces people are most often serene and peaceful, despite their afflictions; they surmount obstacles by their qualities of love, goodness, and forgiveness that would inundate others.

Neptune is the planet of beauty and mystery, and as it rules Pisces, you will be rather aloof from life at times, a daydreamer, and closely allied to all the strange and mysterious forces that rule the universe. You will have a vibrant and magnetic personality that attracts people to you. You are fond of nature, trees, flowers, and oceans, but you are also practical and can adapt yourself to business procedures, finances, and things connected with commerce and industry. Many Pisceans become writers, artists, singers, musicians, and actors. Others turn to the business world and become successful in their own businesses, as they are supersalesmen and have an almost hypnotic effect on those they are trying to sell. By taking advantage of this trait in the Pisces character, you may be able to amass a considerable fortune through salesmanship.

Famous people born in Pisces include statesmen George Washington, James Madison, William Jennings Bryan, and Andrew Jackson; authors James Russell Lowell, Victor Hugo, Henry Wadsworth Longfellow, Elizabeth Barrett Browning, and Edna St. Vincent Millay; Luther Burbank; Chopin; and actresses Ellen Terry, Lillie Langtry, and Elizabeth Taylor. Some other famous Pisceans born in our century are Mike Mansfield, John B. Connally, Robert Lowell, Mickey Spillane, Dinah Shore, William L. Shirer, David Dubinsky, and Jean Harlow.

2

What Profession Should You Choose According to Astrology?

You have been given definite characteristics by your birthsign which fit you for certain occupations and professions. However, it must be remembered in astrology that "the stars impel, they do not compel." Often a person born in a sign that would make a good surgeon might also make an excellent general in the army, as Mars rules both of these professions. Moreover, if a person is born in Aries, ruled by Mars, he has a different character from a person born in Scorpio, also ruled by Mars. The Aries-Mars person could succeed in any field requiring qualities of leadership, endurance, and responsibility. The Scorpio-Mars person functions better in the realm of ideas and promotion, and although he might choose surgery or the military profession, it is doubtful if he would function on just one plane of action. He might become the head of a hospital, or become involved in executive branches of the military rather than in the field, as Scorpio is usually best suited to mapping strategy and outlining courses of action for subordinates.

In giving the various possibilities in the professions for each of the twelve signs of the zodiac, keep in mind that if you have NOT selected the occupation best suited to your sign of the zodiac, you can apply the characteristics given you by your own sign to whatever field you have chosen and still become a great success. For instance, the sign of Gemini often gives one great ability in the field of communications, writing, television reporting, electronics, advertising, but if you choose merchandising or mechanical work, you can use your Gemini qualities to best advantage by knowing your potentials and then aiming your star-given qualities in the direction of creative expression of your Gemini nature. You might wind up thinking up some new form of advertising utilizing newspapers or television that would feature your services or your product to best advantage.

PROFESSIONS BEST SUITED TO THOSE BORN IN ARIES

As Aries rules the intellect, you are best suited to any profession where you can use your higher intellectual faculties. Aries is also the leader, and those born under its influence are aggressive and willing to assume responsibilities. Therefore, you would excel as an executive or boss in any line of endeavor.

Men born in the sign of Aries are often interested in becoming doctors and surgeons. They have a special aptitude for the healing arts and might express their abilities in fields related to medicine, such as psychology or psychiatry. They often select some specialized branch of medicine dealing with the head, eyes, ears, nose, and throat, as Aries rules these parts of the body.

The women make good pediatricians, but the Aries-born are by no means limited to the medical profession. Both men and women born in this first sign of the zodiac also have great artistic and creative talents, and many become outstanding in the creative arts. They are gifted in music, acting, and dramatic writing for stage, television, or screen. They make excellent interior decorators and designers. They have vision and imagination, and when this is applied to the creative arts they often become famous and rich.

The men born in Aries also often show a remarkably creative talent in mechanics. They like electronics, radio, television, aviation, electrical engineering, architecture, and the building trades.

The professions Aries should avoid are those dealing with dull, routine, boring work, or jobs where they are required to do the same thing hour after hour in monotonous and unimaginative work. They can succeed as accountants, but they prefer the challenge of meeting people and becoming involved with the business scene that is always changing day by day and which requires alertness and the use of their excessive vitality and energy.

PROFESSIONS BEST SUITED TO THOSE BORN IN TAURUS

Being born in the second sign of the zodiac which rules wealth, finances, investments, real estate, and material possessions, your first choice of profession would be in a field where you can use your excellent money and investment sense.

Many Taureans have made fortunes in the field of finance and industry, including Winthrop Rockefeller and William Randolph Hearst.

The Taurus-born seldom choose the legal or medical professions. Although they could excel in any profession that requires patience, determination, and tenacity, they are usually better in work that requires imagination and creativity. They often go into real estate and make excellent builders, contractors, and land developers. They often succeed in agriculture, animal husbandry, and raising or training dogs.

However, despite the fact that you have excellent money sense, you are not limited entirely to the above professions. Your ruling planet is Venus which governs all that is beautiful, artistic, and creative. The second choice for the Taurus-born is in the artistic and creative fields. Perhaps more singers were born in this sign of Taurus than any other. Taurus rules the throat and vocal area, and it is small wonder that many of our modern popular singers were born in this excellent money sign, including Bing Crosby (who showed a typical combination of the artistic and commercial instincts of his sign by making a fortune estimated at $700,000,000 through his business acumen), Pat Boone, Kate Smith, Shirley Temple, Dean Martin, Carol Burnett, and Barbra Streisand. Taureans make excellent actors and speakers. They can succeed in any profession requiring use of the voice or through the creative medium of words in print. Many Taureans become successful authors, including Dr. Benjamin Spock, Katherine Anne Porter, Daphne du Maurier, Philip Wylie, and Archbishop Fulton J. Sheen. And, of course, one of the greatest dramatists of all time, Shakespeare, was born in this talented and creative sign.

PROFESSIONS BEST SUITED TO
THOSE BORN IN GEMINI

As your sign is one of the most talented of all in the zodiac, it may be difficult for you to choose your life work. In fact, you are likely to change your mind several times before selecting your profession, and even then, when you seem to be set in one career you may suddenly veer off in an opposite direction and reverse your chosen course for something totally different in nature. You must strive to choose your profession with one aim in mind—choose something that will not prove boring to your changeable nature. There must be variety, continual change, meetings with new and interesting people, and most important of all, work that engages the higher creative mental faculties.

Gemini women make excellent teachers, but they generally do not remain in this position until they retire, often changing to another occupation within a period of from three to five years. Routine work is definitely not for you, but find a career in which you can use your multifaceted personality, preferably in something creative and artistic.

Gemini women seldom choose nursing, as they do not like suffering and pain, preferring an atmosphere of lightness and gaiety. The men in this sign often become lawyers, doctors, and businessmen.

Gemini, being ruled by Mercury, the planet that governs the higher mind, is a sign of talent in the creative arts; many Gemini people choose the field of communication, radio, TV, stage, motion pictures; sometimes they become proficient in writing, directing, and producing. They are also good in the musical fields as performing artists, composers, or symphony directors.

Many Gemini men choose sports as a creative outlet for their talents, and sometimes are proficient in baseball, football, and even prizefighting. Gene Tunney, former world boxing champion, was a typical Gemini with a highly educated mind, and yet he chose sports for his ultimate goal. Joe Namath is another Gemini who made good in the sports world.

But it is in the field of diplomacy that Gemini shows its best side; this can include a business dealing with the public, politics, foreign travel, and being a representative for some large organization. James Farley was a typical Gemini, and he ran political campaigns for some of the biggest politicians, including President Franklin D. Roosevelt; John F. Kennedy became president because of his charm and magnetism; Secretary of State Henry Kissinger is typical of Gemini with his boundless energy, his ability to make important decisions quickly, and the versatility he has shown in meeting with world leaders and scoring important diplomatic gains.

Geminis are supersalesmen in the field of ideas. That is why they excel in advertising, television, and radio communication. The boundless youth and energy of Dr. Norman Vincent Peale, author of the best-selling *The Power of Positive Thinking*, have won him status in the field of speaking, writing, and television and radio appearances. David Rockefeller and Laurance Rockefeller, both Geminis, were able to use their inherited fortunes to build their own financial empires.

Yes, indeed, if you were born in Gemini, the sky is your limit and you can choose any profession that interests you and reach the top, as well as make a very large fortune.

Others born in the talented sign of Gemini were John Wayne, Sir Laurence Olivier, Hubert H. Humphrey, Dr. Paul Dudley White, Brigham Young, Walt Whitman, Ralph Waldo Emerson, Richard Wagner, Herman Wouk, and Sir Arthur Conan Doyle.

PROFESSIONS BEST SUITED TO THOSE BORN IN CANCER

Your sign is noted for its imagination and creativeness. When you choose your life work be sure it is in something that gives your creative imagination full scope. You excel in planning and overseeing big ventures that often encompass large groups of people and big sums of money. The first John D. Rockefeller, who built the financial empire that bears his name, was a typical Cancerian. He had the vision and imagination to foresee the vast industrial growth of America and make provision for its industrialization by producing oil in vast quantities. His grandson, Nelson A. Rockefeller, has not only used his Cancer qualities to increase the Rockefeller fortune, but he made good in the political field as governor of New York for fifteen years. The political field is an excellent one for Cancer people to succeed in. They have vision, courage, and organizing ability to handle many diverse interests.

See the number of people who have used their Cancer talents to achieve success in public work: President Gerald R. Ford, Senators Mark O. Hatfield and George McGovern, George Romney, Henry Cabot Lodge, Thurgood Marshall, and Lawrence O'Brien.

Cancer-born women excel as teachers and nurses. They also make excellent secretaries, salesladies, and personnel directors. Many of them go into interior decorating with success; they often excel in cosmetology and in selling cosmetics, jewelry, and home furnishings to women.

Cancer men do well in businesses dealing with the sales of real estate, stocks and bonds, insurance, or products for the home, such as furniture, household appliances, TV, and kitchen furnishings.

However, the Cancer-born are NOT limited to the above occupations. See the diversity of talents shown by the following Cancerians, and realize that you too can excel in almost any profession you choose: sportsmen Leo Durocher and Jack Dempsey; writers Ernest Hemingway, Walter Kerr, Helen Keller, Ann Morrow Lindbergh, Jean Jacques Rousseau, Pearl S. Buck, and Nathaniel Hawthorne; industrialists John D. Rockefeller, Senior, and John Wanamaker; astronaut John Glenn; and composer Gian-Carlo Menotti. The Duke of Windsor was Cancer-born, as were actors James Cagney, Barbara Stanwyck, and Olivia de Havilland.

PROFESSIONS BEST SUITED TO THOSE BORN IN LEO

The Leo qualities of personal magnetism and leadership fit you for a very high position in life.

The main thing for you to remember in choosing your life work is to get into a job where you can rise to the top. If it offers no chance for advancement do not take it, for you will only be wasting your great talents.

You may start out working under someone else, but you will eventually wind up being the boss! You are best suited to your own business, no matter how small, for it will expand until you build a solid business with a big yearly income.

Medicine and law are the two leading professions for those born in Leo. Many Leo-born make good business administrators, supervisors, and managers of any type of business dealing with the general public. Henry Ford was born in Leo. They are well suited to deal with people and make excellent salesmen, for their charm and magnetism are almost hypnotic in persuading people to buy the products they are selling.

In the field of the arts and business, writing, acting, music, composing, creative art, interior decorating, mechanical designing, architecture, building and contracting, land development, and real estate are all excellent fields for the Leo-born.

Study the following list of talented Leo people both past and present to grasp the wide range of interests that you could become active in and then choose the profession that interests you the most: Ralph Bunche, Arthur Goldberg, Whitney Young, George Meany—all used their Leo qualities to rise to the top in positions of political leadership. Casey Stengel, Willie Shoemaker, and Ben Hogan excelled in the field of sports. In the theater such outstanding stars as Ethel Barrymore, Norma Shearer, Peter O'Toole and Lucille Ball were born in Leo. And, of course, Leo-born often make outstanding authors. Such famous writers as George Bernard Shaw, Sir Walter Scott, John Galsworthy, and Ogden Nash were born in this lucky sign.

PROFESSIONS BEST SUITED TO THOSE BORN IN VIRGO

If you were born in the earth sign of Virgo with the planet Mercury as your ruler, you have a very highly developed mind and should be in work where you can exercise your intellectual faculties.

Virgo women make good teachers and instructors. The men seldom go into this profession; they prefer law, engineering, accounting, advertising, or technical work dealing with scientific research in the chemical, automotive, or medical fields.

Virgo is the sign of patience, adaptability, and detail. Virgos do well in any field that requires a retentive memory, concentration, and infinite detail. The women often seek out positions where they can become supervisors, as they make excellent managers of restaurants, beauty parlors, and apartment houses. They excel at work requiring them to deal with people.

If you are Virgo-born and have a desire to become a creative writer, you can easily achieve success in this field. Your planet Mercury rules the higher intellect and people born in this sign often become writers of fact or fiction. Here is a list of the writers born in this talented sign: Leo Tolstoi, Bret Harte, O. Henry, Upton Sinclair, H. G. Wells, Theodore Dreiser, William Saroyan, F. Scott Fitzgerald, H. L. Mencken, and Robert Benchley.

Virgo-born are naturally behind-the-scenes people, and tend to be modest, retiring, and reserved. Seldom do they become actors, singers, or musicians, although they have talent for these fields; Greta Garbo, one of the greatest stars of the screen, was a Virgo.

Examine the following list of talented people born in Virgo to gain an idea of your own capabilities: Lewis B. Hershey, Roy Wilkins, Alfred G. Vanderbilt, Lyndon B. Johnson, Melvin Laird, Walter Lippmann, Arnold Palmer (noted golf champion), Elliott Roosevelt, George Wallace, Grandma Moses, Walter Reuther, and from the historic past, William H. Taft, Queen Wilhelmina, Margaret Sanger, Marquis de Lafayette, and Cardinal Richelieu.

PROFESSIONS BEST SUITED TO THOSE BORN IN LIBRA

Libra-born are enormously talented in a creative and artistic way. The women born under the sign of Libra and ruled by the beautiful planet Venus are especially suited to work that engages their higher creative minds. Libra women make good actresses for they usually have attractive features, pleasant smiles, beautiful eyes, and most of them are expressive, emotional, and capable of transmitting beauty in the personality and through the voice. Many of the great actresses of the past were born in Libra, including Eleanora Duse and Sarah Bernhardt. In more recent times such stars as Greer Garson, Deborah Kerr, Janet Gaynor, Carole Lombard, Miriam Hopkins, and Helen Hayes were Libras.

As this sign is ruled by the symbol of the scales, Libra people have tremendous mental and emotional balance. The men often choose the legal or diplomatic professions for careers, as they are fluent speakers and dynamic personalities. The magnetic personality with which nature has endowed the Libra-born makes them excellent salesmen, especially if they deal in products that involve beauty products, home furnishings, jewelry, fashion designs, interior decorating, or art.

Libra is shown as the sign of social service and usually, in addition to their regular chosen professions, we find Librans doing voluntary work for the betterment of social conditions. Many Librans are dedicated to social and racial justice. Eleanor Roosevelt and Mahatma Gandhi were Librans.

As Libra is the seventh sign in the zodiac, ruling the house of marriage and partnerships, it is found that Libra people work best in association with others. They make good partners in any business that requires cooperation and adaptability. They are natural peacemakers and thrive in an atmosphere of harmony. They make good labor leaders or mediators. They are honest and trustworthy and should be in work where they can use their high sense of integrity and justice.

Both men and women born in Libra have a great sense of the value of words. They make excellent teachers, ministers, and public officials, as they know how to present an argument, or influence and persuade the public.

If Libras choose the literary profession they have some very good models of the Libra-born who have had great success in this field: Faith Baldwin, Eugene O'Neill, Truman Capote, Jimmy Breslin (newspaper columnist and TV commentator), playwright Arthur Miller, and Thomas Wolfe.

Check the following list of Libra-born to see the versatility and variety of professions that Libra people may select from: William O. Douglas, James Farmer, William Paley, Charles Percy, Arthur Schlesinger, Jr., Mickey Mantle, Wayne Morse, David Ben-Gurion, and from the more distant past such notables as Nietzsche, Admiral Lord Nelson, Franz Liszt, Max Schmeling, and Presidents Chester A. Arthur, Zachary Taylor, and Rutherford B. Hayes.

PROFESSIONS BEST SUITED TO THOSE BORN IN SCORPIO

Scorpio is ruled by the planet Mars and many Scorpio men go into the medical and military fields, professions that Mars is said to rule. The Scorpio women often choose nursing and make a great success of it. However, the Scorpio talents are not limited to the healing arts. This is probably one of the most talented of all the signs in the zodiac, and the Scorpio-born can fit into any of the following occupations and professions: mechanical work, electrical engineering, transportation, and communications such as TV, publishing, and advertising. They are also good in financing, stocks and bonds, investments, real estate, banking, and sales work. The Scorpio-born are good politicians; Robert Kennedy was born in this sign.

Because Scorpio is such a volatile and energetic sign it is best for those born under it to go into occupations where they can work off some of the fire and steam given them by their ruling planet Mars. They like to be the boss and do not take orders well in subordinate positions.

They often rise to the top with their qualities of determination, love of power, and enjoyment of luxury and the good life that money can buy. The Scorpio-born have a healthy respect for money, knowing that it represents power, and they are never satisfied at the bottom rung of the ladder of success. They must rise to the top, and this ambition often makes them seem ruthless, cruel, and aggressive. The Scorpio-born often make many enemies through these traits of pugnaciousness, sarcasm, and desire for revenge; these qualities must be curbed if Scorpios want lasting success.

Other Scorpios who have achieved success are Billy Graham, W. Averell Harriman, Sargent Shriver, Jonas Salk, poet Marianne Moore, Will Rogers, Theodore Roosevelt, Admiral Richard E. Byrd, King Edward VII, Presidents James Garfield and James Polk, Robert Louis Stevenson, Macaulay, Martin Luther, Samuel Insull, Madame Marie Curie, and Ignace Paderewski.

PROFESSIONS BEST SUITED TO THOSE BORN IN SAGITTARIUS

The sign of Sagittarius is ruled by the benevolent planet of good fortune, Jupiter. Perhaps this is why more famous people in every profession were born in this well-balanced and talented sign than in any other except Aquarius.

The typical Sagittarius person is easygoing, kindly disposed, compatible with his coworkers, and in every way a cooperative, honest, and positive individual. Sagittarians fit into almost any occupation where they can use their natural qualities of charm, magnetism, benevolence, and independence. They are natural-born leaders in any field that interests them. The sign rules the ninth house in the zodiac, having to do with travel, philosophy, religion, and the intellect. That is why most Sagittarians are highly idealistic, love to travel, and show an independent and progressive spirit. Sagittarians often do work connected with travel, such as operating a travel agency or conducting tours to foreign countries.

Both men and women born in this lucky sign do well in the financial and investment fields, including the stock market, banking, insurance companies, and higher finance. They make good executives and are dependable, honest, and trustworthy. The keyword for Sagittarius is independence. They do not like work that ties them down to a routine or that is boring and detailed. They have creative minds and often become inventors, writers, artists, composers, and performers in the theater and motion pictures.

However, it is in the fields of finance and industry that most Sagittarians excel. They often build vast fortunes through perseverance, willpower, and determination. It is interesting to note that two of the world's richest men of the past and present, Andrew Carnegie and J. Paul Getty, were born in this money sign.

The danger that most Sagittarians face in building great careers comes from their restlessness and inability to stick with a career that is slow in developing. They want instant success, and sometimes they make changes at the most inopportune times and lose out on what might have been a wonderful chance for advancement.

Look over this list of Sagittarians and be encouraged in your own career by their noteworthy achievements: Sir Winston Churchill, Erskine Caldwell, William Buckley, Jr., Strom Thurmond, Shirley Chisholm, Ramsey Clark, Joe DiMaggio, James H. Doolittle, Margaret Chase Smith, John V. Lindsay, Adam Clayton Powell, Fiorello LaGuardia, Mark Twain, Drew Pearson, Gustave Flaubert, James Thurber, Spinoza, John Milton, Thomas Carlyle, Noel Coward, Willa Cather, Arthur Brisbane, Ludwig van Beethoven, King George VI of England, Benjamin Disraeli, President Martin Van Buren, and John Greenleaf Whittier.

PROFESSIONS BEST SUITED TO THOSE BORN IN CAPRICORN

Capricorn is noted for its qualities of determination and tenacity. Persons born in this sign never give up trying to achieve the top and they often get there, sometimes with little talent, but with great powers of persistence and even stubbornness.

Capricorn people are best in work dealing with facts and figures. They are hardheaded realists. They like to be top man in whatever profession they choose. They make good as accountants, bankers, and real estate and insurance salesmen. They can often rise to the top of their chosen occupation because they are ambitious, hardworking, and stubbornly determined to succeed. Many Capricorns have been called loners, because they are suspicious of others, and sometimes seem ruthless, brushing aside all objections and obstructions with a complete disregard of how they may hurt the feelings of others.

Two examples of Capricorn ability to handle money are those of Aristotle Onassis and Howard Hughes. Onassis, once a deckhand on a Greek tanker, rose to become one of the world's largest shipowners through his great business acumen. Howard Hughes, who inherited half a million dollars, parlayed it into a billion dollar fortune.

The Capricorn-born are excellent businessmen and women. They can become computer operators, engineers, architects, politicians, heads of investment and financial institutions, statisticians, research specialists, bankers, accountants, and lawyers. They seldom choose the medical profession or the arts as a career, although many of them become writers, actors, and singers. Elvis Presley was born in Capricorn, and his determination to succeed made him one of the biggest money-makers of all time in the movie industry.

Study this list of other successful Capricorn people and let it inspire you to succeed in your own chosen profession: Barry M. Goldwater, J. Edgar Hoover, Floyd Patterson, Mohammed Ali (noted prizefighter), James Farmer, and Pierre S. DuPont of the DuPont chemical fortune. Also, from the past, are these famous Capricorn-born: Sir Isaac Newton, Benjamin Franklin, Rudyard Kipling, Joseph Stalin, Alexander Hamilton, William Gladstone, Woodrow Wilson, Helena Rubinstein, Ava Gardner, Gladys

Swarthout, Louis Bromfield, Jack London, Alexander Woollcott, and the youthful-appearing Marlene Dietrich who is typical of the indestructibility of Capricorns.

PROFESSIONS BEST SUITED TO THOSE BORN IN AQUARIUS

If your birthsign is Aquarius you can be a success in almost any profession you choose. Yours is one of the most talented of all signs, and if you heed a few warnings about your sign, you can not only become famous but enormously rich.

Generally speaking, Aquarians do not choose fame; fame chooses them. They seldom struggle, as do the Capricorns, to reach the top; they are elevated by circumstances in their lives over which they seem to have little control. They are often helped by people who recognize their star-given talents and want to assist them in rising to the top of the ladder of success. This does not mean that they can get to the top without some effort, but it does mean that Aquarians seem to have a way of bending people and circumstances to fit their own aspirations and needs.

I recall when Clark Gable first came to Hollywood from the New York stage. His wife, Josephine Dillon, a voice teacher, was struggling to keep him going until he could get a contract. I was called to her home one day to meet the young Gable and to give him my famous Magic Circle which helped people become stars. I saw no great talent in Gable, nor did I see any great desire to become famous, but everyone who touched his life seemed galvanized into frenzied efforts to help him become a star. When he achieved stardom, he quickly found a glamorous society woman and severed his connections with his first wife. Aquarians can often be ruthless and ambitious to succeed through the efforts of others, and they must be cautious not to show disloyalty towards those who have helped them climb to success.

Aquarius is called the sign of the waterbearer, for Aquarians seem to be constantly pouring out their genius and talent to help the world. In this way they are fitted to many different professions. They work best in the glare of the public spotlight and make good politicians, public servants, and executives. They have a flair for showmanship in their personalities, and they are magnetic, warm, and sympathetic. They often help those who are struggling and sometimes are for the underdog. President Franklin D. Roosevelt, a typical Aquarian, overcame every type of personal defeat and reached the top through the loyal efforts of his friends, his political allies, and his wife Eleanor.

It is interesting to note that the Gabor sisters, Eva and Zsa Zsa, were both born in this fascinating sign of Aquarius, and with little talent and the help of many important people, they have achieved not only high goals and a big income but great popularity and success. Aquarians can make it to the top with their natural qualities of charm, magnetism, and shrewdness.

Aquarians have remarkable memories and excel in any work where they must depend on inspiration, memory, and intellect. They seldom have to study hard, as they absorb facts easily and seem to have the ability to recall everything they have ever read, seen, or heard. They make good scientists, inventors, writers, horticulturists, businessmen, investors, and electronics experts. Edison was born in this lucky sign, as were Charles Lindbergh, Artur Rubinstein, General Omar Bradley, Norman Mailer, astrologer Evangeline Adams, James Michener, Louis Nizer, S. J. Perelman, Norman Rockwell, Jersey Joe Walcott, Dean Rusk, Ronald Reagan, Adlai Stevenson, Gertrude Stein, Tallulah Bankhead, Lana Turner, Jack Benny, James Joyce, John O'Hara, Admiral Hyman Rickover, General Douglas A. MacArthur, Jackie Robinson, and from the past, Charles Dickens, Lewis Carroll, Mischa Elman, Robert Burns, Lord Byron, and of course, Abraham Lincoln, probably one of the most outstanding examples of the immortality that Aquarians can achieve.

PROFESSIONS BEST SUITED TO THOSE BORN IN PISCES

Pisces is a dual sign represented by two fish, one swimming upstream, the other downstream. So, too, Pisceans are inclined to have more than one occupation or profession in a lifetime.

The women make good nurses, teachers, and secretaries. They are also fine musicians, singers, and actresses. Neptune, which rules this sign, is said to rule the shadow world, including motion pictures and TV, as well as drugs and the sea.

The men in Pisces often become chemists, chemical engineers, druggists, radiologists, and sometimes doctors in specialized fields.

Many Pisceans work in occupations connected with oil or the sea, making good investors in stocks dealing with oil or working on board ships as navigators and captains. They are also good in institutional work, caring for the elderly and poor. They are good in occupations dealing with foods, and often make good caterers, chefs, dietitians, and managers of restaurants or food processing plants.

Pisceans are known to have the proverbial "green thumb," and they generally love plants and growing things. They make good in the fields of agriculture, botany, and horticulture. Luther Burbank was born in the sign of Pisces.

The Pisces-born usually make friends easily and are good in any work where they are required to meet the public. They are sensitive and have good intuition, sensing how to win people and how to hold their friendship and interest. They have an almost hypnotic power over the minds of others and are good in selling any products dealing with cosmetics, beauty, the home, and home furnishings. The women are also good as cosmetologists and in the field of hair, skin, and body care.

Check the following list of Pisceans and draw inspiration from the fact that these famous people had your same star-given talent and destiny and used it to achieve greatness, riches, and fame: Mike Mansfield, John B. Connally, David Sarnoff, Edward M. Kennedy, Mrs. Richard Nixon, Harry Belafonte, David Dubinsky, William L. Shirer, Dinah Shore, Elizabeth Taylor, Mickey Spillane, Earl Warren, Robert Lowell, Robert Taft, Jr., John J. McClellan, and Linus Pauling.

Then consider the famous Pisceans of past history and realize that this sign can be ranked first among those who had great potential for fame and fortune: George Washington, James Madison, William Jennings Bryan, Andrew Jackson, James Russell Lowell, Victor Hugo, Henry Wadsworth Longfellow, Elizabeth Barrett Browning, Chopin, Enrico Caruso, Henrik Ibsen, and Nikolai Rimsky-Korsakov.

In summing up your potential for your sign of the zodiac, realize that there is no particular line of work that you must follow. You have freedom of choice in the matter, but your stars do incline you in certain directions and it will be much easier for you to succeed in your chosen vocation if you know your possibilities and your limitations. If you are in work that is not listed for your sign and you enjoy it, by all means do not give it up. You will succeed if you use your star-given character to make the most of whatever particular field you have chosen in which to express your talents.

3

Your Star Guide to Happiness in Love and Marriage

It is a pitiful commentary on our modern age of permissiveness in love that three out of every five marriages end in divorce. If it were only the marriage partners who were concerned it might not be so bad, but children of such unions are often emotionally disturbed through the ugliness of divorce, and their own lives reflect the patterns of emotional instability that they witness in their parents.

Astrology is a certain guide to love and marriage happiness. The stars give tendencies and characteristics which can be determined by any person before entering into marriage. There are certain compatible signs and others that are incompatible.

In this chapter you can learn about the signs of the zodiac that are compatible to you in love and marriage. You can avoid the incompatible signs and save yourself heartaches and disappointments. And if you find that you *are* married to someone of the wrong sign, you can take steps to know your mate's true character and then work harder to overcome the elements of dissension and build a more solid union for the future.

Despite the fact that many people marry people of the wrong sun signs, they may have elements of compatibility elsewhere in their charts which give harmony. For instance, the moon position is very important in considering the right marriage partner, but as the sun is the most powerful planet in our astrological system, we are here concerned only with its planetary position at time of birth.

COMPATIBLE SIGNS IN LOVE AND MARRIAGE FOR THE ARIES-BORN

If you were born in this fiery sign, ruled by the planet Mars, you have to be extremely careful in love and marriage. You will be your own worst enemy for with your tendency to impatience, quick temper, and desire to dominate, you are often very hard to get along with.

Because you have such a deeply emotional nature and love is so essential to your life, you should choose your love and marriage partner with the greatest caution. You are apt to be possessive, jealous, and suspicious of your mate. You demand absolute loyalty on the part of the beloved, although you are inclined to wander and flirt, even when married. This is something that you must avoid if you want to have absolute happiness in love and marriage.

When you do attract the right love partner, you can be ardent, loyal, and you make a good parent. You enjoy the comforts of the home and you make a good lover, as you are emotionally intense and passionate.

Five things to do in love and marriage if Aries-born:

1. Forget you were born in the dominating sign of Aries and try to adapt yourself to your mate's needs.
2. Try to remember your mate's emotional needs.
3. Remember your mate's birthdate and anniversaries.
4. Try to have daily discussions about your love or marital problems rather than dominate your beloved.
5. Show more affection and at least two times a day, say the three little magic words that keep love alive, "I love you."

Your most compatible signs are:

1. Leo. This is a fire sign also and one that is very strongly attracted to you. However, the Leo-born are sometimes self-centered and inclined to want to dominate, so be sure that you can tolerate such a strong, dominant sign before marrying.

2. Sagittarius. This is also a fire sign and one that can be very compatible to Aries. But there are warnings about typical Sagittarians: they are usually freedom-loving people, so when they marry they expect it to last for life as they are giving up their independence. Respect their love of freedom and do not hold the reins too tightly; allow them to have their own friends and some personal activities which you do not share and you will get along beautifully with Sagittarians.

3. Libra. This is your opposite sign and it rules the seventh house of marriage and partnerships in the zodiac. Libras make good marriage partners for Aries for they are loving, kind, considerate, and unselfish. However, they are very sensitive and easily hurt and you might have to learn to curb your Aries temper and show more kindness and love. Many astrologers do not believe in marrying an opposite sign, but in my extensive experience I have found that they often have the most enduring marriages.

4. Gemini. This sign, like Libra, belongs to the air trinity, and fire and air signs form highly volatile unions which are often stormy and cause many problems, but when these are worked out satisfactorily, such unions last and the marriage partners are never bored with each other. As they get older, their love grows stronger.

Your incompatible signs are Cancer, Pisces, Capricorn, and Virgo.

You can have romantic alliances with Taurus, Aquarius, and Scorpio, but marriage is not recommended with these three signs.

COMPATIBLE SIGNS IN LOVE AND MARRIAGE FOR THE TAURUS-BORN

Your sign is ruled by the planet of love and beauty, Venus. You are a natural lover and are highly sensitive to the overtones of kindness, sympathy, generosity, and consideration in your love life. Your emotional needs are very great and you love a home, children, and all the positive things that marriage offers.

Taureans make wonderful parents and are gentle and generous towards the members of their family. However, because you are so sensitive and dislike disharmony, you must make a great effort to attract a mate who can give you a peaceful, harmonious, and beautiful home environment and plenty of love.

Your most compatible signs are:

1. Virgo. This is an earth sign and ideally suited to your passionate and loving nature. Virgos may appear cool and reserved on the surface, but once you win their love you will have a mate who is forever loyal, loving, and devoted.

2. Capricorn. This sign is also an earth sign, and it has integrity, solidity, and perseverance, qualities that your Taurus nature admires. Capricorns are also successful, and women born in Taurus who want a good husband, father, and provider would do well to choose a Capricorn husband. The women born in Capricorn are good organizers and managers; they run a good home and often help the husband in business. They make good wives.

3. Cancer. This is a highly emotional sign. Cancerians love children and the home. Cancer men make the best husbands for Taurus women, as they are gentle, considerate, and loving.

If you are a Taurus man, you can choose a Cancer woman as your wife, for they make the most wonderful mothers and they are loving, kind, and gentle. They are highly emotional and can make a Taurean happy for a lifetime.

4. Pisces. This is a water sign and an ideal mate for the earthy Taurean. Pisceans are emotional, warm, generous, and kind. A Piscean loves the home and children and can match the Taurean for loyalty and devotion.

The incompatible signs to avoid in marriage are:

1. Scorpio. They are inclined to be too dominating and jealous.
2. Leo. They are often self-centered and too positive.
3. Sagittarius. They are too independent and strong-willed.
4. Aquarius. They are often insincere and inconstant in love.

COMPATIBLE SIGNS IN LOVE AND MARRIAGE FOR THE GEMINI-BORN

Gemini is one of the most demanding of all signs in the zodiac in love and marriage. Owing to the dual nature of this sign, it is often difficult for the marriage partner to understand a Gemini. You must choose most carefully if you want to find happiness in love and marriage for your volatile and changeable nature makes it difficult to find love and marriage happiness.

Your most compatible signs are:

1. Libra. This is an air sign and strikes the happy balance between the physical and mental needs of the Gemini-born.

2. Aquarius. Perhaps no other sign of the zodiac understands Gemini as well as does the Aquarian. This sign, ruled by the planet of originality and imagination, Uranus, is capable of bringing happiness to the Gemini-born. Although there will always be problems between these two signs, when these are ironed out and the wild Aquarian is domesticated, Aquarius can be one of the best of all signs for love and marriage with a Gemini-born.

3. **Sagittarius.** This is your opposite sign in the zodiac and it is said that "opposites attract but also repel." There is strong magnetism between Gemini and Sagittarius, but there are danger signs which must be carefully watched. With a Sagittarius lover or mate, do not be jealous or possessive. Let your Sagittarian lead the way in domestic matters. Learn to be lighthearted and gay with your Sagittarius mate, as they do not like moods and the heavy atmosphere which Geminis sometimes adopt.

Incompatible signs for the Gemini-born are Capricorn, Virgo, Scorpio, and Aries. They can often have romantic alliances with Taurus, Leo, and Pisces, but these are not marriage signs in the truest sense of the word. They are good for romantic alliances, business, or friendship only.

COMPATIBLE SIGNS IN LOVE AND MARRIAGE FOR THE CANCER-BORN

Yours is a very sensitive and emotional sign, and the Cancer-born often make tragic mistakes in their choice of a marriage partner. For instance, if you choose an Aries or a Leo, you are doomed to unhappiness and may wind up in the divorce courts.

Your sign makes you loyal and loving, and you are a natural parent. This house in the zodiac is said to rule the home and the intimate circle of your close family connections. It is vitally important that you choose and marry the right marriage partner if you want to fulfill your destiny perfectly.

Your compatible signs are:

1. **Pisces.** This is a water sign, like yourself. Pisces people are deeply emotional, possess beautiful minds, and are ideal mates for the tempestuous Cancerians.

2. **Taurus.** The steadfastness and loyalty of a Taurus mate will give you the stability you need emotionally. Taureans make good love and marriage partners because of their loyalty and love of a home life. If you want to attract a Taurus mate, show love and affection and enter into the activities that please Taureans.

3. **Scorpio.** This belongs to the water trinity of the zodiac. Scorpios are noted for their loyalty and devotion when married to the right person. Being ruled by the fiery planet Mars, they

supply the energy, vigor, and fire that can make a union with Scorpio ideally happy but at times a little tempestuous. You can win Scorpio by being loyal, devoted, and by not showing jealousy.

4. Virgo. This is a very fine earth sign and is suited to you because it has the cool reserve and fine emotional control which your sign often lacks. Virgos give balance to your sign, and as they love the home, children, and the joys that marriage can bring, they can be ideally suited to you.

If you were born in Cancer, it is good to avoid marriage with those born in the following signs:

1. Aries. They are apt to be too dominating and selfish for a sensitive Cancerian.

2. Sagittarius. This sign is likely to be too independent and strong-willed for you to take.

3. Gemini. This is a sign of duality and strange restlessness which would only add to your confusion and uncertainty.

4. Leo. Leo-born are charming people but NOT for Cancerians as they are too self-centered and dominating.

COMPATIBLE SIGNS IN LOVE AND MARRIAGE FOR THE LEO-BORN

The sign of Leo, ruling the fifth house in the zodiac, has to do with love affairs and children. It is in the department of love that Leo excels. You are a natural-born lover and enjoy conquest of members of the opposite sex. This sometimes leads to quick romances and marriages and sad awakenings. If you marry the wrong sign you will not hesitate in getting a divorce, so it is good to study the compatible and incompatible signs for you.

Your compatible signs are:

1. Aries. This is a fire sign and matches your ardor, affection, and loyalty when really in love. Not that there won't be problems if you marry an Arian! Arians are often stubborn, demanding, and self-centered. They may compete for the spotlight with Leo, but they are your match, can satisfy your emotional needs, and give you an exciting, joyous, and fulfilled life.

2. Sagittarius. This ninth house sign is also a member of the fire trinity to which Leo belongs. Sagittarians make wonderful lovers and marriage partners. They are loyal and sincere. They are honest and seldom cheat on their mate. They are lovers of freedom and if you give them free rein they will never stop loving you and sharing in the joys of a warm, companionable, and romantic relationship.

3. **Aquarius.** This is the sign opposite to Leo, and has much to offer to a union with that sign. Aquarians are easy to hold if you understand their aspiring, lofty, and idealistic natures. They thrive on love, adulation, and flattery. A Leo-born can handle this strong, dominant sign. The Aquarians are dreamers and have grandiose plans that perfectly fit in with the Napoleonic complex that many Leos have. The conqueror Napoleon is typical of the confidence possessed by this sign. The Leo-born can conquer the hearts of anyone they meet.

Incompatible signs for the Leo-born are Gemini, Cancer, Pisces, and Scorpio. Leo can have friendships and romances with Libra, Taurus, Capricorn, and Virgo, but these are not recommended for marriage.

COMPATIBLE SIGNS IN LOVE AND MARRIAGE FOR THE VIRGO-BORN

Virgo people are very particular in the choice of a marriage partner. They may have romances with any sign of the zodiac, but they must be very cautious as to which sign they select for that important step. As Virgos are highly discriminating, critical, and demanding, they must have a mate who understands them and who can live up to their idealism and perfectionism. Virgos make the most wonderful mates when married to their right signs.

Your compatible signs are:

1. **Taurus.** This is an earth sign, like yourself, and it offers stability, emotional reciprocity, and loyalty in love and marriage.

2. **Capricorn.** Although this sign is somewhat cold and reserved, Virgos have what it takes to warm them up! You will like the determination to succeed that Capricorn has. You will also like their loyalty and devotion.

3. **Cancer.** The water signs are compatible to earth signs, but this sign is more compatible than Scorpio. You need the warmth, affection, and devotion that can be given you by a Cancer mate. They love the home and children, as you do.

4. You can also marry a Piscean, another water sign that has

great compatibility, even though it is your opposite. This sign has great emotion, warmth, and loyalty and makes an excellent lover or mate for those born in Virgo.

Incompatible signs are Scorpio, Sagittarius, Leo, and Libra.

COMPATIBLE SIGNS IN LOVE AND MARRIAGE FOR THE LIBRA-BORN

As this sign is ruled by the planet of love, Venus, it is vitally important that you select a marriage partner who suits your rather exacting needs.

First, a word of caution for you if you were born in Libra. You are apt to be in love with the ideal of love and you may wear your heart on your sleeve. You believe everyone who says they love you and you are inclined to let your romantic idealism blind you to a person's true character. Many Librans marry in haste and repent in leisure. To avoid this misfortune, study carefully the list of those signs most compatible to you.

Your compatible signs are:

1. Aries. Oddly enough, this fire sign that is opposite your sign in the zodiac is a powerful and magnetic sign for you in love and marriage. But there are warnings: you must be prepared for the dominating nature of the Aries-born, also for their quick tempers and impatience. They get over their outbursts quickly, and they make great companions, being fun-loving, romantic, and tireless in their boundless enthusiasm for life.

2. Gemini. As this is also an air sign, it furnishes you with a compatible element. Gemini possesses the versatility, changeability, and intellectual capacity that constantly intrigue and hold your interest.

3. Aquarius. Here is a highly emotional, volatile, and magnetic sign which can make you an excellent lover and mate. You are both humanitarians and you both like the same kinds of music, art, and literature; you enjoy dancing, parties, and a gay social life. Aquarius can lead you on a merry chase and bring you security, fame, and fortune.

The incompatible signs are Scorpio, Capricorn, Sagittarius, and Virgo.

Many Librans have made happy marriages with those born in

Taurus, a sign also ruled by Venus, but care must be used in choosing this sign, as Taureans are often dominating, stubborn, and strong-willed. If you select a gentle, intellectual, and loving Taurean, this can be considered a compatible sign.

COMPATIBLE SIGNS IN LOVE AND MARRIAGE FOR THE SCORPIO-BORN

Your sign rules sex magnetism and the sensual impulses, and all Scorpios have a strong sexual drive. It is important that you select a mate who is able to satisfy your love requirements and marriage rather than a sign that is cold, aloof, and sometimes sexually indifferent which is apt to lead you to break up.

Your compatible signs are:

1. Pisces. This is a water sign and matches your warmth and ardor in love. Pisceans are loyal and not overly possessive. As your sign is somewhat possessive and jealous of your beloved, you must be careful not to hurt your overly sensitive Pisces mate with suspicions and accusations of infidelity.

2. Cancer. The typical Cancer mate is a very wonderful partner in love and marriage. Cancerians love the home and children, as you do. They are inspiring and encouraging and push their mates in the direction of success and achievement. You will find Cancer warm, responsive, and sexually mated to your sign in every way, giving long-lasting love, affection, and fidelity.

3. Capricorn. As this belongs to the earth trinity, it can be said to be compatible to the water sign of Scorpio. You will like the Capricorn drive to success and you will have much in common romantically, as this sign can be very loyal and passionate when it is mated to its true soul mate.

Sometimes the opposite sign of Taurus is compatible to Scorpio, but great care must be taken to avoid the stubborn, strong-willed Taureans who might want to dominate you and drive you in their direction. If you attract the gentle, loving, and sensual Taurean who lets you have your own way, you can make a success of marriage with this sign.

Incompatible signs for Scorpio are Aries, Leo, Libra, and Scorpio. These signs might be good for casual friendships and romances, but they are not enduring enough for the permanency of marriage.

COMPATIBLE SIGNS IN LOVE AND MARRIAGE FOR THE SAGITTARIUS-BORN

Your love nature is warm, affectionate, and loyal. It is imperative that you make the right choice in a marriage partner, for when you give up your freedom for the married state you are giving up something very precious to a Sagittarian. You have much to give to a marriage as you are cooperative, loving, and deeply affectionate. You love children and make sacrifices for your mate and your children.

Your compatible signs are:

1. Leo. This sign is of the fire trinity and suits you in ardor and loyalty. Leo people are generally able to understand your love of freedom and they will not hamper your own expression of creativity in a career or your independence. They love children and make excellent parents.

2. Aries. This fire sign is also a compatible one for Sagittarius. Arians are natural-born leaders, and you will enjoy their sense of humor and eternal optimism. Try to find an Aries who is of the same intellectual background as yourself, so that you will have a great deal in common.

3. Gemini. This sign is your opposite and attracts you strongly because of the magnetism it has for you. However, here is a word of caution about Geminis. You must be prepared for their moods, changeableness, and split personalities. They make ideal mates if you can understand their erratic and restless natures.

4. Aquarius. Strangely enough, this air sign is often very compatible to Sagittarius. Aquarians are understanding and are advocates of freedom; they will let you have your own way most of the time. They are good lovers and emotionally suited to you. They are temperamental, idealistic, original, and creative, and these qualities all suit your sign perfectly. You would furnish the balance that these Aquarians often need to make them happy in marriage.

Sagittarians actually can get along with almost any sign of the zodiac as they are so adaptable and conform well to the needs of others. There are some signs, however, that would not be good in the marriage state with your sign; these are Cancer, Scorpio, Taurus, and Capricorn.

COMPATIBLE SIGNS IN LOVE AND MARRIAGE FOR THE CAPRICORN-BORN

More than any other sign in the zodiac, your sign needs love and understanding. People often misunderstand the typical Capricorn person because of his dignity and natural reserve. They are apt to think of you as being cold, unemotional, and unresponsive. You are quite emotional and responsive to love and kindness and long to find your true soul mate. However, you are ruled by Saturn which often causes delays in love and marriage, and you sometimes do not find the right marriage partner early in life. I know many Capricorns who did not until they were thirty or even forty. Some choose to remain single throughout life, as did J. Edgar Hoover.

Your compatible signs are:

1. Taurus. This sign is affectionate, loyal, and especially suited to your sign as Taureans belong to the earth trinity and love the home and children. A combination of Taurus and Capricorn makes for a happy union in every respect.

2. Virgo. This is also an earth sign and has the ability to adjust easily to the Capricorn temperament and needs. A union with Virgo brings peace and tranquility in the home, emotional reciprocity, and loyalty.

3. Cancer. This is your opposite sign in the zodiac and can furnish the magnetic and emotional polarity which you need to keep you emotionally interested throughout your marriage. Cancer mates adore children, make good parents, and are loving, kind, and warm human beings.

4. Pisces. You can easily adjust to water signs and Pisces is one of the best for you. Pisces has the neutrality needed for one with your strong, dominant character. Pisceans like to help a Capricorn mate reach the top of the ladder of success.

Incompatible signs are Scorpio (although a water sign, it is apt to be too dominating and jealous for your nature), Gemini, Libra, and Aries.

COMPATIBLE SIGNS IN LOVE AND MARRIAGE FOR THE AQUARIUS-BORN

Your sign is the most romantic and idealistic of all signs in the zodiac. You seem to be in love with love and you are always searching to find the ideal love or mate. Unfortunately, this often leads to fickleness on your part and may involve you in as many as two or even three marriages. People born in this sign can get along fairly well with all signs of the zodiac for Aquarius can be all things to all men, but some are more suited to you than others. The Gabor sisters, John Barrymore, Clark Gable, and Lana Turner were Aquarians who had several spouses, so you can see the tendency with Aquarians to keep searching for the ideal mate. Franklin D. Roosevelt, although married to his ideal, Libra, in Eleanor Roosevelt, had fickle tendencies, according to his biographers.

Your compatible signs are:

1. Gemini. I put this sign first because in Gemini you will find the mental and intellectual equal to your sign. Also, you admire fluent conversationalists and interesting and original personalities, and Gemini is all of that.

2. Libra. This is an air sign and ideally suited to the temperamental and fickle Aquarian. Libra is the sign of balance and often exerts a very steadying influence on Aquarians. Libra is a very beautiful sign, not only mentally but often physically, and Aquarius admires these qualities above all others in its mate.

3. Leo. This is the opposite sign in the zodiac from Aquarius, and often makes a very satisfactory mate. Aquarians like a witty, fun-filled marriage partner, and Leos are magnetic, charming, and know how to win and hold the love of an Aquarian.

Signs incompatible to Aquarius are Scorpio, Sagittarius, Cancer, and Virgo.

COMPATIBLE SIGNS IN LOVE AND MARRIAGE FOR THE PISCES-BORN

Your sign is one of the easiest to get along with in the entire zodiac. Any sign can really unite with you and achieve unity, love, and happiness, for yours is a neutral sign that blends harmoniously with most of the other signs of the zodiac. However, your best and most compatible signs are:

1. Scorpio. This sign, ruled by the fiery planet Mars, suits your calm and placid nature as you like fireworks occasionally. The Scorpio mate is loyal, affectionate, tempestuous, and passionate. They are capable of intriguing you with their magnetism and charm. Richard Burton was born in this sign.

2. Cancer. This sign is temperamentally and emotionally suited to your own Pisces nature. You enjoy the comforts of a home and you love a family. The Cancerian is able to share in this passion with you and together you can create a beautiful home environment and a romantic marriage that should bring few problems.

3. Virgo. This is your opposite sign in the zodiac, but it has great magnetic and romantic attraction to you. You like the dependability of Virgo; you like their honesty and integrity. They, more than any other sign of the zodiac, can help you overcome your duality and develop a strong, decisive personality that keeps you from going into opposite directions at the same time, like the two fish which symbolize Pisces.

Incompatible signs to Pisces are Aries, Leo, Sagittarius, and Libra.

Taurus is very often compatible to your sign if the Taurean is the intellectual type and not the earthy, typically stubborn Taurus.

4

How the Stars Affect Your Children and Their Destinies

There are three vital forces that affect your child and his destiny. These are:

1. Heredity
2. Environment
3. Education

These forces can mold and shape a child in ways that affect his character and react on his destiny.

However, there is a fourth influence on your child which people are now beginning to be more aware of than ever before. This is the effect of the stars on your child at the time of birth. The stellar influences modify and affect heredity, education, and environment. A child's inner drives and motivations are often star-given, and to know your child thoroughly and to be able to help him shape his future more intelligently, it is important that you understand his star-given character and destiny.

If, for instance, your child is a Capricorn and you want him to become a doctor or surgeon, you are going to be in for some disappointments. It is unlikely that your child will show much interest in the studies and hard work necessary for the profession of medicine. His interests lie in another direction: in the field of business, finance, even aviation. He will be happier as a merchandising expert or a business tycoon than as a doctor.

Now, don't get me wrong. Many Capricorns have become doctors, and probably under parental pressure, but the point is they would probably have been happier in some other profession.

Your child might be a Gemini, ruled by the planet of the mind, Mercury. You might want him to be a mechanic and work in a garage on cars. But his interests are more on the mental and creative plane. He could apply his talents to being an architect, an engineer, an aviator, or even a television technician, but he would be out of place working as a mechanic and would soon tire of it and try something else.

Study the influences that existed at the time of your child's birth. Get to know his inherent strengths and weaknesses, his hidden potentials for greatness. Then aim his training and education in the direction of his star-given talents and he will achieve his true destiny.

If you are now planning a future family, you have it within your power to select the actual star-given destiny that you want your child to have. Study the following facts about each of the twelve signs and how they affect your future child, and then you can consciously select the time of conception that will, in nine months' time, produce a child who will be born in the sign of the zodiac you have selected. This will give you power to mold his destiny and select his traits and characteristics, so you will be happier than if your child were born in a sign that is unfavorable to you and your mate.

THE DESTINY OF YOUR ARIES CHILD

Your Aries child is unusually fortunate in that he will be given tremendous vitality and creative energy and can rise to any heights he chooses. There are, however, certain weaknesses in this sign which you should be aware of and which you can help your Aries child overcome.

For instance, Aries children are strong-willed, stubborn, and dominating. They will quickly try to take the lead in your family circle, and if there are other children who were born in weaker signs, your little Aries child will soon manipulate them in his direction. You can use tact and love in handling him, but you should avoid force and physical punishment.

You will find your Aries child takes an interest in everything around him at a very early age, but it is in a curious way; he likes to take things apart to see what makes them work. He is interested in all forms of electronics and mechanics, especially if they make loud noises. His toys are likely to be taken apart quickly, and if you give him mechanical gadgets to play with, be sure they make a noise. This is hard on the mother, but will keep him amused for hours.

This trait is what makes your Aries child fit for occupations concerning mechanical things, heavy machinery, factories, and punch presses, where there is noise, confusion, and action. His ruling planet is Mars, and he will like all things connected with war: toy tanks, trucks, soldiers, and battlefields. If your Aries is a little girl, she will be interested in more refined things: dolls that walk, talk, and can be fed and changed. She will show natural nursing ability at an early age and may want to become a nurse when she grows up.

Keep your Aries child busy; devise games he can play, social activities that encourage him to refine his aggressive and combative tendencies. When he reaches the age of understanding, talk to him and reason with him as he has a sharp, intelligent mind and can be reached easily with logic. When he shows streaks of bad temper, which he will do often, do not raise your voice and shout at him, for he will enjoy this and will fight back; lower your voice, adopt a calm manner, and talk rather than scold. He will respond to love and kindness more than to force or disciplinary action.

Aries children will show their natural tendencies and aptitudes for their future life work early. Boys born in this sign work well with their hands. They enjoy working in the field of radio, television, electronics, and aviation. They are good soldiers and soon rise to the highest level if they have had preparatory education. The Aries-born should be encouraged to go in for higher education, or if they don't they should be encouraged to take a specialized course of training that will prepare them for their life work.

Aries girls are apt to be restless and changeable. They show romantic interest early in life and often marry before going into higher education. They make good nurses, teachers, accountants, and saleswomen. Many Arians, both girls and boys, show an early tendency to become creative artists, actors, musicians, and singers. Some of them could be trained to become actors and achieve great success. Such noted stars as Gloria Swanson, Charlie Chaplin, Joan Crawford, Bette Davis, and Spencer Tracy were born in Aries.

As Aries is said to rule the brain, your Aries child may show tendencies to great brilliance in his studies, and learn things quickly, but he is also apt to lose interest just as quickly and want to go on to something else. His nature is aggressive, changeable, adventuresome, and impulsive. You will have to work hard to keep him on his chosen path for he will have a tendency to try his hand at everything and succeed at nothing if he is not controlled.

THE DESTINY OF YOUR TAURUS CHILD

Your Taurus child will give you much pleasure and enjoyment, for he likes the home and is happiest when surrounded by loving members of the family. Ruled by Venus, the planet of love and beauty, he is apt to be gentle, kind, and generous. He will have to be trained to take care of his money since being overly generous, he is inclined to spend money easily, mostly on his friends or buying gifts for members of his family.

Taureans can be quite obstinate at times, and they cannot be pushed in any direction they do not choose. They have excellent reasoning faculties and can be appealed to through the facts rather than through emotional pressures.

Your Taurus child has a natural leaning towards the arts and creative work. He can be trained to become an artist, fashion designer, interior decorator, architect, musician, singer, or actor. However, most Taureans do not go in for the theatrical life as they are usually modest and retiring.

Taurus, being an earth sign, gives natural talent to Taureans for real estate, agriculture, botany, and horticulture. They are also good as veterinarians and breeders of fine cattle.

Because this is a very diversified sign, many Taurus-born take to the field of literature and make fine writers of fiction or factual books. Shakespeare, Charlotte Brontë, Karl Marx, Archbishop Fulton J. Sheen, and Dr. Benjamin Spock were all born in Taurus, showing what a wide range of subject matter attracts Taurean writers. Taureans also make good newspaper reporters and television announcers.

Taurus, being the house in the zodiac having to do with money, also fits your child to become a financier, banker, investment broker, or real estate agent. Taureans are usually most successful in dealing with tangible things from the earth and they often make a fortune through financial investments, especially in real estate.

THE DESTINY OF YOUR GEMINI CHILD

You are fortunate in having a child born in this fascinating and versatile sign. You will never cease to marvel at his multifaceted personality. He will learn to speak and walk with ease, probably earlier than most children. He will show a remarkable memory and is highly imitative. You can mold his young mind in any direction you choose, for Geminis are very versatile and adaptable.

Always remember that your Gemini child is a dual personality; it's almost like having twins in your home. He may show one side of his personality one day and a completely different side the next. He should be handled carefully, not giving in to his demands when he is in his imperious and demanding moods. He will respect you if you are firm and keep to your word.

Because your Gemini child is dual in nature, he will also have dual talents; in fact, one of his main problems will be in choosing his right life work for he will be interested in many different things.

His sign gives him certain talents that are outstanding, and yet, he can go against his star-given talents and choose something quite different and original.

The planet Mercury, the ruler of Gemini, has to do with communications: television, writing, speaking, teaching, or training salesmen. The Gemini-born are at their best when they have to use the medium of speech or the written word to convey their thoughts and ideas. They are highly intellectual and can make good in writing, art, advertising, interior decorating, and the performing arts. They also make supersalesmen.

Many Gemini men go into law and some follow up with a political career. Hubert Humphrey and President John F. Kennedy were born in this interesting and talented sign.

Many Gemini women become fine teachers and instructors, often rising to supervisory positions as they are diplomatic and know how to handle people. They are good in any position where they have to meet the public, such as hostesses or reception secretaries.

Many Gemini men turn to the sports world and become skillful in baseball, boxing, or managing athletes. Gene Tunney, former world boxing champion, was born in Gemini as was Joe Namath.

Some very fine writers have been born in this mentally gifted sign, including Dr. Norman Vincent Peale, Herman Wouk, Terence Rattigan, and from the past, Sir Arthur Conan Doyle, Ralph Waldo Emerson, Julia Ward Howe, and Walt Whitman. This sign may rightly be called the sign of the genius, as Geminis can develop their minds to high levels of inventive and creative action that often bring them world fame and wealth.

THE DESTINY OF YOUR CANCER CHILD

Your Cancer-born child is ruled by the planet moon, and like the moon which is continually changing, so, too, the Cancer-born like to work where they can change their routines frequently and follow a variety of interests.

Your Cancer child will be extremely sensitive and reflective. He may show tendencies to being quiet and studious. He is easy to discipline with a word or a gesture as he responds to parental authority without the struggles of an Aries or a Scorpio child. The main thing to know about your Cancer child is that he may be subject to moods and hypersensitivity. Try not to scold him too often; avoid giving him an inferiority complex by telling him of his inadequacies. Praise him a good deal and try to instill a positive attitude towards life and people.

As Cancer rules the home, children, and things pertaining to women, Cancer girls usually select nursing, teaching, or a profession where they can sell objects for the home. They are also excellent in cosmetology, beauty products, and jewelry. Cancer women have great minds for detail, and make excellent legal secretaries, dental assistants, salesladies, and personnel directors.

Your Cancer son will show great interest in a higher education and may select law for his profession, or he may want to become a financier or business administrator. Many Cancer men make good as certified public accountants, and some go into the stock market as brokers and investment advisers.

Seldom do Cancer men choose the medical profession, but if they should, they usually become pediatricians, psychiatrists, or psychologists. They are good at helping people solve problems and are sympathetic, kind, and compassionate.

Your Cancer child will not be interested in money for its own sake, but he likes to be a success so he can do things for his family or for the public. The first John D. Rockefeller was born in this good money sign, and his Rockefeller Foundation has helped thousands of people through its scientific and medical research. Many Cancer men choose public service and work in federal or state government. They make honest, reliable, and efficient public servants. Nelson A. Rockefeller, grandson of John D. Rockefeller, was born in the sign of Cancer, as were also these public servants: Calvin Coolidge, George McGovern, George Romney, Henry Cabot Lodge, Gerald R. Ford, Mark O. Hatfield, and Thurgood Marshall.

In considering occupations for your Cancer-born child, do not neglect the creative and artistic. If he shows leanings towards the arts, having the imaginative moon as his ruling planet, he could achieve outstanding success as a writer, artist, musician, composer, or inventor.

THE DESTINY OF YOUR LEO CHILD

If you have a Leo child in your family you can pat yourself and him on the back and praise yourself for bringing him into the world in one of the luckiest and most wonderful signs in the entire zodiac.

If you still do not have a Leo child but can arrange events so his birth will fall between July 22 and August 23, in the sign called Leo, you should do so without fail. A Leo child will bring you great personal happiness and satisfaction and will undoubtedly achieve a great destiny.

Now, this does not mean that Leo children are not without faults. There are certain things you as a parent can help them avoid as they mature. They are inclined to be self-centered and sometimes selfish. If there are other children in the family, your Leo-born will want to take center stage and keep it, resenting it when you pay attention to the others in the family.

Your Leo child can be a tyrant and try to push others around to suit his will, for this strongest of all signs is given vitality, energy, and a sense of domination. The symbol for Leo is the lion, king of the jungle. Your Leo child will have a strongly developed ego, great personal magnetism, and charm and will be able to win the support and love of everyone he meets. He expects to possess the world and all therein. Remember that three great conquerors who changed the course of history were born in Leo; they were Alexander the Great, Julius Caesar, and Napoleon. Don't give in to your Leo child's every whim, and occasionally say "No" to his demands and he will build a stronger character.

It is impossible to put Leos into any given category for talent for we find their brilliance, their exploits, and great achievements in every known field. They excel in the professions of medicine and law. They become big politicians and often achieve power and dominance over others. They make the best businessmen in the world. They dominate the field of music, acting, and writing.

Your Leo child will show certain preferences very early in his career. Let his own intuition guide him to the choice of a career. Do not try to force him into any category, but let him find his own way, giving him encouragement and support of his own opinions about his future work. Give him a college education, if possible, for when he is fortified by a diploma he will be able to forge his way to the top as a business executive, investment expert, lawyer, politician, in the fields of land development and real estate, or as manager and head of any large business organization where he has many people working under him.

Many outstanding actors and writers were born in this talented sign, including Mae West, Lucille Ball, George Bernard Shaw, Edna Ferber, James Baldwin, and Ogden Nash. The sky is the limit with your Leo-born child!

THE DESTINY OF YOUR VIRGO CHILD

Virgo is considered a practical, hardworking, and highly intelligent sign which gives qualities of patience, precision, and endurance to the character. Your Virgo child will be studious and eager for schooling, as Mercury is his ruling planet and this governs the intellect.

Your Virgo child will be highly moral and aware of his duty and obligation not only to his family but to the community at large. That is why they often make good public servants and choose the fields of medicine, nursing, teaching, and social work.

The men make excellent lawyers for they are methodical, painstaking, and detailed in their thinking. They present a good appearance, being neat, clean, and well-groomed. The Virgo women are often very style-conscious and are excellent fashion designers and interior decorators. Very often the women born in Virgo become dietitians or work around foods.

Your Virgo child will be pleasant and agreeable and will listen to you carefully before making up his own mind. He has very few bad qualities to overcome except that he may be overly shy and introverted. To make him socially aware, encourage him to play games with neighbors' children and to mix with others.

Virgo children often appear indolent or indifferent, and seem to escape from reality. They are natural daydreamers, and when in such moods they are usually on flights of imagination in which they are building a mental world of their own. This should not be encouraged too much, and yet it should not be altogether discouraged, for Virgos have very active imaginations and these mental exercises often indicate that your Virgo child is destined for a career in music, acting, or literature. The planet Mercury gives them great proficiency in the arts, and some Virgos become great artists and designers. See the list of famous people born in this gifted sign and you will realize that your Virgo child also has the potential for greatness.

Grandma Moses, the noted artist who began painting in her seventies, was born in Virgo, as was Jane Addams, who became famous as a social worker. Humorists H. L. Mencken and Robert Benchley were also born in this talented sign, as were writers Theodore Dreiser, William Saroyan, Leo Tolstoi, Walter Lippmann, and F. Scott Fitzgerald.

However, your Virgo child also fits into the more prosaic and practical realms of business, such as pharmacy, law, teaching, accounting, scientific research, aviation, and electronics.

Give your Virgo child a good education, college if possible, and leave the rest to him. You will be proud of him.

THE DESTINY OF YOUR LIBRA CHILD

If you have a child born in this fortunate and beautiful sign, you probably already know that he will live a charmed life. Venus, the ruling planet of Libra, often makes Librans charming and attractive. The women are usually quite beautiful physically and possess good figures. They are proud and enjoy wearing beautiful clothes and being admired. Their traits can sometimes lead to excessive vanity and a desire for constant love, attention, and adoration. When this is not forthcoming they are apt to feel neglected. To be married to a Libra woman is often difficult, so you must train your Libra girl to be practical and not expect constant praise.

Your Libra boy will be charming also, but not so vain. However, being ruled by Venus, he will like the easy life and may develop qualities of laziness or irresponsibility early in life.

Libra is symbolized by the scales and the Libra-born are often delicately balanced between the mental and physical. They are outwardly peaceful, calm, and cool, but they may be inwardly emotionally turbulent and easily unbalanced by any crisis or sudden shock. They must be trained to have mental control and to adapt themselves to the changing fortunes of life.

Libra girls have natural artistic and creative minds. They make good fashion models and actresses. They are also good in designing jewelry and making smart clothes for women. They excel in the field of cosmetics, and are often makeup experts in television and motion pictures. As Venus, the planet of beauty, is the ruling star, they are good in any work that has to do with beauty, the home, and decorations.

Nursing is not to be encouraged for the Libra-born, as they are sensitive and do not like to see human suffering. However, they make excellent social workers and teachers, and have a streak of the humanitarian in them. Eleanor Roosevelt was a typical Libran. Although not beautiful, as most of them are, she had an inner spiritual beauty that shone in her personality and made her magnetic and charming.

Libra men seldom follow the artistic professions. They make good lawyers, judges, and public workers. We see examples of this among such Librans as William O. Douglas, James Farmer, Wayne Morse, Arthur Schlesinger, Jr., Charles Percy, Mahatma Gandhi, David Ben-Gurion, and Dwight D. Eisenhower.

As a writer of poetry or fiction, your Libra child could achieve fame and fortune if trained in that art. Some famous writers born in Libra are Faith Baldwin, Jimmy Breslin, Truman Capote, Arthur Miller, Eugene O'Neill, and Thomas Wolfe.

Libra women often make very fine actresses. Eleanora Duse and Sarah Bernhardt were born in this sign.

THE DESTINY OF YOUR SCORPIO CHILD

Scorpio is one of the strongest and most vital signs in the zodiac, and your child will have a rugged, strong body and vigorous good health. You can consider him capable of fighting his own battles in life and of rising to great heights in his future career.

Ruled by the fighting planet Mars, your Scorpio child will have a strong will and a quick temper. He may show signs of his independence and strong will early. Do not try to break his spirit or bend his will to yours; work patiently and calmly to harness his tremendous energies and his capacity for getting into mischief. If he is a boy, furnish him with outlets for these energies when young by devising games and sports.

If you have a Scorpio girl, she will be less active, but she will still be tremendously vital and filled with a desire for fun and mischief. Give her dancing or music lessons. Let her dabble in art as a creative outlet for her vital mental energy.

Both Scorpio girls and boys may show early tendencies to become doctors and nurses. They are natural healers, sympathetic, kind, and considerate.

Your Scorpio child must learn early in life to curb his tendency to sarcasm and quarreling. He may not get along with his brothers and sisters; he may want to dominate them and subject them to his control. He must be disciplined with firmness, but never with physical punishment, for this makes him rebellious, resentful, and desirous of revenge.

The base side of Scorpio is suspicious, revengeful, sarcastic, and dominating. This is represented by the symbol of the scorpion that can sting its victims.

The loftier side of Scorpio is represented by the eagle which can soar to the heights of inspiration and achievement. Strive to give your Scorpio child high ideals and goals. Teach him to curb his tendency to stubbornness and anger and transmute it to higher realms of creative effort.

Evangelist Billy Graham is typical of the type of Scorpio who has risen to great heights in his humanitarian work. Jonas Salk, who gave his polio vaccine to the world without asking for money, is also one of the eagle Scorpios of our time.

Your Scorpio son may become a doctor, a military man, a mechanic, engineer, banker, investment broker, real estate salesman or developer, or go into the manufacturing and sale of motors, factory equipment, mining or working in metals, or he may even become a great athlete.

Your Scorpio daughter would make a good nurse or teacher. She could also become an excellent executive secretary to a businessman or a lawyer. She has the ability to become a fine saleswoman, dealing in real estate or selling merchandise to the general public. She might also choose some branch of the army, navy, or air force in which to serve and she could be quickly elevated to the rank of captain. Then again, she might choose government service, working in some department of state or federal government where she would soon be elevated to a supervisory position.

THE DESTINY OF YOUR SAGITTARIUS CHILD

Jupiter is the ruling planet of this sign. It is considered one of the most fortunate signs in the zodiac, and Jupiter usually brings a very wonderful future with rich rewards in every department of life.

Your child born in Sagittarius will show his traits of independence and love of freedom very early in life. You may take this for willfulness and obstinacy, but do not try to change him for these are his basic qualities. He will be adventurous and always want to go someplace and do something different. These children of Jupiter are the explorers, travelers, and pioneers of history. Your child will be easygoing, pleasant, and optimistic. He can get along with everyone and makes hosts of friends. He will be lucky in almost everything he undertakes for his nature is cheerful, trusting, and intuitive. People will like him on sight and make his path in life easier than it is for most people.

Jupiter, the planet ruling Sagittarius, is said to govern the public and politics. It rules the ninth house in the zodiac and has to do with religion, philosophy, and intellectual pursuits, as well as travel. Your Sagittarius child would be a good traveling representative for some big business corporation. He would also be good in any business dealing with money and investments, such as banking, the stock market, or merchandising.

The Jupiter-born often choose the political arena and make

great politicians and leaders. Sir Winston Churchill was typical of the Sagittarius-born in his great achievements as a statesman, orator, writer, and artist.

But if the first choice in profession for Sagittarius is business and public work, we must not forget that some of our great writers were also born in this talented sign, including John Greenleaf Whittier, Gustave Flaubert, Mark Twain, James Thurber, John Milton, Thomas Carlyle, Noel Coward, Willa Cather, and columnists Arthur Brisbane and Drew Pearson.

Some other Sagittarians who achieved success in the political field are John V. Lindsay, William Buckley, Jr., Shirley Chisholm, Strom Thurmond, Ramsey Clark, and Margaret Chase Smith.

THE DESTINY OF YOUR CAPRICORN CHILD

Your Capricorn child will be a very strong and dominant personality. You have to adjust to him for he will not easily adapt himself to you. This is a fixed sign and Capricorns are ruled by Saturn which makes them ambitious, determined, and dominating.

This is not to say that your Capricorn child will not be charming and pleasant. He has tremendous magnetism and can make himself most agreeable when he wants to get something out of you, but underneath is the rigid, unyielding, stubborn, and determined character that can make him rise to great heights of achievement.

Your job in rearing your Capricorn child will be to give him guidance and direction when he wants it, and at other times let him choose his own course of action. His hardworking and honest nature fits him for success in fields of industry, merchandising, finance, and investment. He does well in real estate and land development. He is also talented in public work such as state or federal office. He would make an excellent lawyer and public administrator. He is fitted for any work where he must be a leader and way-shower. His serious nature and sense of responsibility make him an excellent lawyer, judge, or civil servant. He has great ambition and aims toward high goals where he can have power and dominance.

He is apt to be a loner and he may not make friends easily. Encourage him to play with other children and indulge in competitive sports and games where he can learn to give as well as take.

The Capricorn-born should be given business training for they are excellent in banking and in any work dealing with figures and finances. They make good research scientists; they are excellent in any kind of work that requires adding machines and computers as they have a talent for figuring out things like interest, percentages, stock accounts, and financial investments.

Seldom will your Capricorn child choose an ordinary occupation; he wants to reach the top of whatever he goes into. He would like to become a big financier, like Capricorn-born Aristotle Onassis and Howard Hughes. Sometimes a Capricorn boy will aspire to the heights in sports, as did Floyd Patterson and Mohammed Ali who were born in this gifted sign.

Two extremes of Capricorn were Stalin, dictator of Russia, and Elvis Presley, the famous singer. Between these two extremes are gifted people in science, literature, politics, and the arts. Study the lives of these Capricorn-born to better understand the vast potentials your child possesses: Benjamin Franklin, Alexander Hamilton, William Gladstone, as well as Presidents Millard Fillmore, Andrew Johnson, and Woodrow Wilson. Then there were noted writers like Jack London, Louis Bromfield, and Alexander Woollcott.

THE DESTINY OF YOUR AQUARIUS CHILD

Your Aquarius child will be especially gifted and will fit into the new Aquarian age, with its marvelous space explorations, atomic discoveries, and great advances in the fields of science, industry, and invention. Not only will he be a humanitarian but he will be born with a mind that is highly inventive, original, and creative.

Some of the world's great leaders and humanitarians were born in this great sign, including Presidents Abraham Lincoln and Franklin D. Roosevelt.

It is true also that more people born in the sign of Aquarius are geniuses and achieve outstanding success in whatever field they choose than those born in any other sign of the zodiac.

Despite all these good things about your Aquarius child, there are certain warnings also. He is apt to be self-centered and have an ego that requires constant praise and admiration. He may develop into a demanding and selfish adult if everyone in the family puts him on a pedestal and praises him constantly. His natural charm and magnetism make him an appealing and irresistible child who can win the heart of any person he meets. This is the fatal charm and also, very often, the downfall of Aquarians for they can rise to the heights but also fall to the depths through their own weaknesses, vanity, and pride.

Train your Aquarius child to be honest, punctual, and trustworthy. He should be taught to work harder to achieve his goals and not depend on friends and relatives to help him. He must be taught the sacredness of marriage and the home, for very often Aquarians are confused in love and marriage, often having two or three marriages and divorces.

The occupations that your Aquarius child is best suited to are technical and electronic work, airplanes and automobiles, engineering and scientific research. Aquarians make good technicians in television and often become inventors and innovators of machines and methods for manufacturing and distributing.

They do not select the field of medicine as often as the legal profession. When they start as lawyers they generally rise to become important in state or federal government posts.

We must not forget the many famous creative and literary geniuses born in this highly talented sign; some of them were Norman Rockwell, Norman Mailer, James Michener, James Joyce, Charles Dickens, Robert Burns, Lewis Carroll, and Gertrude Stein.

Charles Lindbergh was born in the sign of Aquarius, as were Adlai Stevenson, Ronald Reagan, Dean Rusk, and General Omar Bradley.

THE DESTINY OF YOUR PISCES CHILD

If your child was born in Pisces he needs special attention and care if he is to mature as a self-reliant and successful person. Pisces tends to make people vacillating, changeable, and indecisive. They are often indolent and do not like to study or work hard.

Your Pisces child will be a typical daydreamer, and may spend a good deal of time in imagining the life he would like to live without actually taking steps to achieve his goal.

Being born in the last sign of the zodiac, called the house of self-undoing, your Pisces child may be his own worst enemy. He is apt to be dual in nature and not know which side of his nature to follow. He is inclined to be overly sensitive and highly emotional. He reflects those around him and if his parents smoke and drink, the Pisces child will take on those habits. If he gets in with those who are addicted to dope, he is likely to try it and may become hooked. He must be given constant training and supervision until he has reached mental and emotional maturity to be sure he does not become influenced by bad companions when he is young and impressionable.

Your Pisces child would be good in social service work. He is naturally kind, sympathetic, and likes to help people. He is often taken advantage of by his friends and coworkers who borrow money and never return it. Pisces people are always burdened with the sad tales and problems of their friends and often sacrifice themselves for others, even to the point of self-deprivation.

Girls born in Pisces make good nurses, teachers, and welfare workers. The boys make good pharmacists, merchants, salesmen, investment brokers, real estate salesmen, technicians, psychologists, psychiatrists, and marriage counselors.

Your Pisces child was born in good company for some very famous people, past and present, were born in this gentle and talented sign, including George Washington, James Madison, Andrew Jackson, William Jennings Bryan, Enrico Caruso, and Albert Einstein. Also such writers as James Russell Lowell, Victor Hugo, Henry Wadsworth Longfellow, Elizabeth Barrett Browning, and Henrik Ibsen were Pisceans.

In our own age the following were born in Pisces: John B. Connally, Mike Mansfield, Edward M. Kennedy, Mrs. Richard Nixon, David Sarnoff, Harry Belafonte, Mickey Spillane, Dinah Shore, and Elizabeth Taylor.

5

How to Use Astrology to Become Successful and Rich

When you once know your star-given potential for greatness, you can use astrology to guide you to fame, riches, and success.

Each sign of the zodiac has a different path to money and success. Some, like Scorpio, can make a fortune through creative ideas and devising new techniques and methods for selling a product or promoting it to bigger sales.

Others, like Gemini, can use their star-given qualities to delve into the realm of the mind and intellect, and obtain inspiration to achieve fame and fortune through the medium of communications: writing, television production, advertising, newspaper and magazine work, or through business ideas dealing with the sales of some special kind of service, or a sports article, or the entertainment world.

It is through other people that we achieve success and riches. People want your ideas or your products and give you money for them. To appeal emotionally to people and enlist their aid and support is to win them over to your side of the road and have them working to bring you the riches you desire.

Each sign of the zodiac can be reached through a different type of appeal. Some, like Leos, have grandiose ideas and love power. They are hard to influence or sway, but they have an Achilles' heel, as do all signs of the zodiac. When you once discover this vulnerable area through a study of the stars, you will become master of people and you will be able to command and control them so they will do your bidding.

The Open Sesame to fame, riches, and success is your star guide to people's characters. Study each of the twelve signs of the zodiac carefully, as given here, and learn how you can best utilize this knowledge to help you rise to high levels of achievement, power, fame, and riches.

HOW TO MOTIVATE AN ARIES PERSON TO HELP YOU BECOME SUCCESSFUL AND RICH

In dealing with any Aries person keep in mind his star-given character. Your Aries is impulsive, takes an interest in anything new that is presented to him, and often rushes headlong into signing papers or buying a product or service because of its novelty.

To sell an Aries person anything from an insurance policy to a new car, appeal to his desire to be first in everything, to be the leader, to be admired for having a better home, a finer car, a more secure future for his family and himself. Remember that Aries people have a feeling of power and lavishness, and they are extreme optimists when it comes to money; they believe they will continue to have an inexhaustible supply of cash, so they do not mind spending it if they can increase their feelings of expansiveness and power.

An Aries person will reach for his pocketbook for one of two reasons: if he thinks he can gain power or comfort through his purchase or investment, or if he thinks your products or services will show him off to an advantage before other people. The Aries-born respond to flattery of the most blatant sort. Before trying to sell your Arian a service or a product, tell him how you know of his accomplishments, how respected and admired he is among his coworkers and friends. Make him feel that he is number one in every respect and that you are delighted to be able to bask in the warmth of his magnetic personality, his charm and his manliness; or if it is a woman, her beauty. Arians open up like a flower feeling the warmth of the sun when you use this emotional appeal on them.

Then, when you have won the Aries confidence and made him feel you are great to have discovered his true worth, you can present your product or your service to him. Always stress the importance of your Aries being even greater, more perfect, more comfortable, more secure, and more respected by others, through availing himself of your product or your services.

Use the keyword "you" in selling an Arian, and soft pedal the personal pronoun "I."

Key sentences to use with an Aries-born:

"You have achieved something unusual in your work, I hear from your friends and acquaintances."

"You are unique in that you have been able to do what you did."

"You can impress your family and friends by having the new car."

"You and your family can live in the lap of luxury in your old age if you invest in this old-age security insurance policy."

"You want to be admired and respected by everyone you meet, don't you? Then wear this diamond ring (or this suit, or overcoat), and it will make you the center of admiring circles of people who recognize your good taste and good judgment."

IF YOU WERE BORN IN ARIES DO THESE THINGS TO WIN SUCCESS AND RICHES

1. Learn how to hold onto your money and do not let your enthusiasm make you buy things you cannot afford or will soon tire of.
2. Do not yield to the high-pressure salesmanship that makes you feel you must have the expensive car, jewelry, or clothing that you may not yet be able to afford.
3. Avoid "get-rich-quick" schemes in oil, gold, uranium, or speculative stocks, and put your money into solid investments like real estate or land, income units, or a home that may grow in value over the years.
4. Learn to curb your impatience in your desire to become successful and rich, and realize that you must grow slowly but surely in any business or financial venture.
5. Try to go into your own business, no matter how small it may be, as you make money faster working for yourself.
6. Curb your impulsiveness and desire to put on a show and live lavishly. You should never buy things you cannot afford and never live in a house or drive a car that is beyond your means, for indebtedness is the sure way to failure.

7. Establish credit early in life, and borrow money from a bank which you pay off, so you can make bigger loans when you need the money to go into a business or expand your present business. This type of indebtedness is based on sound economy, whereas to go into debt for cars and luxuries only causes you to sink deeper and deeper into a financial rut from which it will be difficult to extricate yourself.

HOW TO MOTIVATE A TAURUS PERSON TO HELP YOU WIN SUCCESS AND RICHES

It is not easy to separate a Taurean from his money or to influence him quickly to buy your product or your services. Taurus rules money, as this is the second house in the zodiac dealing with finances, investments, real estate, and speculation.

To capture the interest of a Taurean, do NOT flatter him as you do the Aries-born. The Taurean will see right through your flattery and know you are trying to get something out of him.

To engage his interest and attention, talk to a Taurus man about his business, his future prospects for success, and about money in general. He is interested in stock-market investments, in property for income and growth, and in any product that can add to his income in the future and give him security for his family and himself.

If you are trying to sell a Taurus woman, you can get her interest immediately by talking about her home, her children, and her desire to give her family comfort, security, education, and social advantages. Remember Taurus rules love also, as Venus is the ruling planet, so women born in this sign are interested in romance, beauty, and ways by which they can keep young, look romantic, and hold love forever. If you get on any of these subjects with a Taurus woman, you can sell her just about anything that will help her achieve the above objectives.

Use the following key phrases to influence a Taurean to part with his money:

"Remember, financial security in old age is something most people do not have. You can invest in this policy and it will give you and your family protection in later years."

"Your home and your family life will be vastly improved by investing in this."

"You want comfort, not luxury; efficiency in the car's performance, not outward beauty alone. This car is built to give you economy in operation and performance, and simple, down-to-earth beauty which will give you pride and delight."

IF YOU WERE BORN IN TAURUS DO THESE THINGS TO WIN SUCCESS AND RICHES

1. Make it a point to put part of your money away where you cannot touch it: an annuity that matures when you reach forty or fifty, a savings account that you must leave for two years to draw bigger interest rates, or in real estate that lies on the outskirts of some growing community that will mature in ten to twenty years, giving you security for old age. You grow wealthy by being conservative and using your money wisely.
2. Get into a business where you can handle money or be around money. Banking and the investment fields are good for you to align yourself with.
3. Sell products that deal with beauty and women. You are a natural salesman for such things as clothing, jewelry, cosmetics, home furnishings, and food products.
4. You might consider investments connected with land, such as commodities on the market, oil speculation, gold mines, and uranium if it is possible to put only a small part of your money into these ventures. Taureans often get rich through things from the earth. Cattle raising and farming are also good ways by which you might add to your wealth.
5. Buy a home early in your life, for you must work from a solid base and you will be able to concentrate better on making a success financially if your home life is settled, routine, and comfortable.

HOW TO MOTIVATE A GEMINI PERSON TO HELP YOU WIN SUCCESS AND RICHES

You can appeal to Geminis through the intellect rather than through the emotions. Appeal to their higher natures, their interest in people, in travel, and in the communication of ideas.

Gemini is the sign of the mind and of communication. If you can start a Gemini talking, you can quickly get an idea of his predominant interests and then dwell on these, rather than try to sell him your product or your service. Never let a Gemini feel you are trying to use him to get somewhere, but make him feel that you consider it a privilege to be able to share something with him.

Remember also that the typical Gemini is a dual personality, and you have to be very sure to approach him when he is in a high, bright, optimistic, and expansive mood. He is then generous with his money, talkative, pleasant, and sociable. When he is in one of his dark moods, avoid trying to sell him anything or get him to do you a favor. His mood will pass and you can try again.

Never offer a Gemini two alternatives in trying to sell him a product or a service. Tell him of only one way that it will work or help him. If you give him an alternative path he will vacillate and never sign on the dotted line.

In trying to win or control a Gemini, remember that he is interested in books, education, television communication, travel, and people. You can intrigue him by talking about social concerns, about people in high places, and about the current interests in the fields of art, music, literature, politics, and business. He is alert and up to date on everything, so you have to be very sensitive to his needs and feelings.

Keep in mind some typical Gemini people who are famous and you will have a key to the diversified interests of the Gemini-born: the Duchess of Windsor, partygiver Elsa Maxwell, publisher Bennett Cerf, financier Jay Gould, President John F. Kennedy, Henry Kissinger, Dr. Norman Vincent Peale, and Joe Namath. Now, if you can visualize yourself trying to capture the interest of this diversified group of people, you will realize that you must be up on your toes to be able to interest or hold them or sell them your ideas, your products, or your services.

IF YOU WERE BORN IN GEMINI DO THESE THINGS TO WIN SUCCESS AND RICHES

1. Get into some public work where you can capitalize on your brilliance, your effervescence, and your multifaceted personality. You can get to the top in your life work by associating yourself with people who are educated, cultured, and socially prominent. Your winning personality and magnetism draw others to you, so get into public work where you can use your gifts to convince and

intrigue people in power, and you will be on the high road to riches.

2. Try to cultivate more perseverance and do not change your work or your mind so often. You will find it difficult, but you must stick with something over a period of several years if you wish to achieve the greatest success and become rich.

3. Try to study and develop your natural talents for speaking, writing, and teaching others. You are a master psychologist and a diplomat in handling people. Commercialize on these gifts. If you can get into television production or directing, you can become famous. If you try your hand at writing you can usually make a fortune. Your sign is also famous in fields of music and acting, so perhaps your path to fame and fortune lies in the use of your personality, charm, and talent to win the hearts of the public. John Wayne and Bob Hope did this through Gemini talents.

4. Gemini often becomes rich overnight through an idea for a new business procedure or the creation of a new product or service which can win him a fortune. The Gemini mind is very inventive, so try to devise some new object or method for making your business successful and you may become a millionaire! Revlon's Charles Revson did this through a beauty product. Others did it through discovering plastics and nylon and polyester products. With your Gemini imagination you can find your pathway to fame and riches by discovering something new and different that you can make and sell to the public.

5. If you invest in stocks, try to stick to Gemini fields, which have to do with television, radio, motion pictures, and other mediums of communication.

6. For partnerships or those who work best with your sign choose those born in Libra, Aquarius, and Sagittarius. You have to be careful of working with Aries, Scorpio, and Taurus as they are a little too demanding and dominating for business and money associations.

7. You can rise rapidly in work that requires tact and diplomacy, such as representing a large organization where you make contacts with heads of firms. You are also capable of making money through traveling, as a representative, or working with heads of foreign countries in the diplomatic corps, the U.N., or governmental agencies.

8. What are your chances of owning your own business? They are excellent if you can contact the public and sell them on your personality and charm. Any product, from food to house furnishings, would be good to go into as you are a supersalesman and can usually sell anything to the public.

HOW TO MOTIVATE A CANCER PERSON TO HELP YOU BECOME SUCCESSFUL AND RICH

Always remember in your dealings with Cancerians that these are among the most sensitive people in the zodiac. Handle them with kid gloves and avoid saying things that irritate them. Do not criticize them and find fault with them, but give them kindness, love, and understanding, and you will win them to your side. They are kind, generous, loving, and trusting souls and respond to kindness, courtesy, and gentility.

Cancer people are highly conservative, so you cannot sell them a product or service without their giving it great consideration and thought before buying it. The symbol for this sign is the crab, which progresses by moving sidewise. So, too, your typical Cancerian finds it difficult to make a definite decision, and never commits himself without hedging and stalling. If you try to get money out of them, it is practically impossible unless you use a certain type of appeal.

As Cancer rules the fourth house in the natural zodiac dealing with the family and home, you can always appeal to their protective and love instincts for their family. They will do anything for their marriage partners and their children. You must show them how it will benefit their families, how it will improve their home and their families' comfort, health, or well-being, and you will have appealed to their hearts and pocketbooks.

Cancerians are great worriers about the future; they fear every type of calamity from going insane to going broke. If you can give them reassurances of security, safety, sanity, financial growth in the future, they will listen to your sales talk and respond with alacrity. These are highly imaginative people, and you must appeal to the high quality of emotion that is engendered when you call up visual images of the good things your product or your services will do for them.

IF YOU WERE BORN IN CANCER DO THESE THINGS TO WIN SUCCESS AND RICHES

1. Overcome your tendency to be excessively conservative and take a chance at times on an investment or a business venture that is presented to you. After checking it thoroughly, force yourself to take a stand and be determined that it will be a success. This positive attitude will get rid of your vacillation and sidestepping of issues that often cause you to lose a golden opportunity to become rich or famous.

2. If you decide to go into a business of your own, choose the restaurant business, where you can sell food and drink at reasonable prices. Your knowledge of what the public wants should bring you a fortune in this business. Also, you can run a hotel or motel. Jack Dempsey, who won fame as a prizefighter, later went into the hotel and restaurant business with great success.

3. With the moon as your ruling planet, you can become rich and successful in any work requiring a high degree of imagination. This could include interior decorating, designing clothes, selling cosmetics or jewelry, or becoming a writer of fiction. Your talent is great and with proper training you could easily succeed in the creative and artistic fields. See the successful writers born in the sign of cancer; they include Margaret Mitchell (author of *Gone With the Wind*), Pearl S. Buck, Kathleen Norris, Anne Morrow Lindbergh, Ernest Hemingway, Nathaniel Hawthorne, and Helen Keller.

4. If you decide to go into the business and industrial world, choose some product that deals with women, the home, or children. You have an instinct for what the public wants and needs and you would be a success in manufacturing or selling anything from toys to washing machines. Retail merchandising is especially good as a Cancerian is good at making sales to the public. John Wanamaker, department store founder, was a Cancer. John D. Rockefeller, Sr., was also born in this sign.

5. Real estate development is especially favored if you were born in the sign of Cancer. You are able to evaluate accurately what property is worth and what you can get for it with improvements. You would also do well in land development, where future growth would make your fortune by selling or subdividing.

6. Another field in which Cancerians excel and often make fortunes is in the antique business by buying and importing antiques

from foreign countries and selling them for a large profit in this country. You have a natural feeling for fine books, good art, and valuable antique furniture and could undoubtedly make a great deal of money in this field.

HOW TO MOTIVATE A LEO PERSON TO HELP YOU BECOME SUCCESSFUL AND RICH

Always keep in mind the Leo personality: he has grandiose ideas, loves flattery and attention, is self-centered and egotistical, and responds to people who cater to him and his needs. You can win the attention of any Leo person if you show you are completely enamored of him, his charm, his personality, his looks, and his importance. The Leo must be the center of focus in your attempts to win him and influence him in your direction.

If you are trying to sell something to a Leo person, always emphasize how its possession will make him more attractive and outstanding in the eyes of his friends and family and how it will bring out his superior qualities. If it is a new car, do not dwell on its functioning in a superior way but stress how people of his caliber always choose a car that is superior in workmanship, design, and beauty and how it will make people admire his superior intellect and good taste in having selected that particular car.

If you are trying to sell a Leo a new home, do not stress its comfort, gardens, or accessibility to schools, but dwell on how he can entertain his important friends, how he can shine like a jewel in a beautiful setting, how he can make contacts with important people who will admire him for having selected such a beautiful home to live in. In other words, build up the ego and self-importance of Leo. They are not worried about future security or how long a product will last; they are very much concerned with how it will give them the edge over other people or how it can add to their importance and public standing. They like recognition and social prestige, and you can get anything you want out of them if you play up these elements. Jacqueline Kennedy Onassis is typical of Leo women.

If you work with a Leo person and your advancement depends on him, you will do well to defer to him in everything. Make him feel superior; turn to him for advice and guidance; play the part of a subservient and dependent person; and act as though you believe the sun rises and sets in your Leo boss. He will soon give you promotions and advancement, whereas if you put him down or fail to pay homage to his superior qualities, he will soon resent you and keep you from ever progressing in your work.

IF YOU WERE BORN IN LEO DO THESE THINGS TO WIN SUCCESS AND RICHES

1. Realize that the sun, your ruling planet, never takes a back seat for any other planet; it dominates our planetary system and gives life to earth. So, too, you must realize that you were born to rule, to dominate, to be a boss and not a worker. You should strive early in your life to get into a position where you can hold a position where others work for you and under you. You should try to get into your own business, if possible, where you can meet the public and exercise your natural charm and magnetism in influencing them to buy your products or services.
2. Also realize you are a person with superpersuasive powers and make a supersalesman. Try to get into a field where you meet important, successful, and rich people. This can be in the investment field, as a stockbroker, or a real estate agent selling big homes or apartment houses to rich people. You can become a lawyer, handling large corporations, but you should avoid criminal law. You can make a fortune as a doctor, especially a pediatrician, treating children of rich people, or a psychiatrist, catering to a wealthy clientele.
3. Yours is such a lucky sign that you can turn your hand to almost any kind of profession and become a big success. You are especially favored in the entertainment world, either as a performer or as a maker of stars. You have the ability to recognize talent and you might get together a singing group, cut records, distribute them, and make a million. Many Leos make good in the television and theatrical field, including Lucille Ball who is estimated to be worth many millions, and Mae West who rose to fame and fortune on her terrific Leo magnetism and little else. In the early days of movies, Norma Shearer, queen of MGM, not only became a great star, but married the head of the studio! Ethel Barrymore was also a Leo of exceptional talent.
4. You are particularly lucky in the political arena, if you are a Leo, for your love of power, your personal charm, and magnetism can

not only win votes, but help you rise to a very high position in that field. Ralph Bunche, Arthur Goldberg, George Meany, Whitney Young, Henry Ford, and Herbert Hoover were born in Leo. And, of course, the notable historical conquerors Napoleon, Julius Caesar, and Alexander the Great were all born in Leo. The ill-fated Mussolini, who used his power unwisely, also was born in this sign of power and dominance.

5. If you want to achieve fame and fortune quickly and with a minimum amount of effort and hard work, you might have a talent for literary work, as your sign is gifted in this field. Frank Munsey, noted publisher, was a Leo, as were Joseph Pulitzer and Charles A. Dana. George Bernard Shaw, Edna Ferber, and Booth Tarkington were also born in this gifted sign.

HOW TO MOTIVATE A VIRGO PERSON TO HELP YOU BECOME SUCCESSFUL AND RICH

Virgo people admire qualities of honesty, hard work, and competence. If you want to appeal to the typical Virgo person, do not tell him you will make him rich overnight or that your product or services will bring him popularity and fame, for he dislikes the spotlight and this will cause him to close up like a clam.

Your appeal to a Virgo must be on a basis of how you can help him do his work better, run his business more efficiently, make more money by using your services, or win security for his family by buying what you have to sell. Virgos are just the opposite from Leos who love ostentation and are show-offs.

Appeal to your Virgo through a sense of honesty and integrity. Keep your promises to one born in this sign; they are generally always on time and they respect a person who keeps his word.

Don't get the idea that your Virgos are all prudes or schoolteachers, or cold and indifferent, as many astrology books claim. They are warm, kindly, responsive human beings, underneath a seemingly cold and suspicious exterior.

You cannot flatter Virgos, as you might an Aries-born, or soft-soap them, as you could a Taurean, for they see through false flattery and do not respond.

The Virgo tendency to be slightly withdrawn and aloof is protective. If you can find a way to break down this barrier you can easily win a Virgo person over to your way of thinking, especially if you are honest about your intentions and have faith in your products and your services.

The Virgo-born respond to wit and humor if it is not obscene or vulgar. Two of our great storytellers, O. Henry and Bret Harte, were born in this gifted sign. So were Upton Sinclair, H. G. Wells, Theodore Dreiser, Leo Tolstoi, William Saroyan, and F. Scott Fitzgerald. And you must also remember that two of our great humorists, H. L. Mencken and Robert Benchley, were born in this sign, so appeal to Virgos through their sense of humor and you will lower their walls of reserve and win them for friends or business associates.

Greta Garbo was a Virgo, and her desire for privacy was one of the keynotes of her character, but once you met Garbo, she could be the most charming and warm human being alive. Gayelord Hauser is another Virgo who has a magnetic personality, and he has made a fortune through writing about health and diet. Incidentally, health, diet, and how he can remain young and slender are some of the predominant interests in a Virgo's life. The women are especially obsessed with new diets. So, if you are trying to win a Virgo and influence him to give you money or position, talk about health, foods, the latest fad diet and you will have intrigued his interest at once.

IF YOU WERE BORN IN VIRGO DO THESE THINGS TO WIN SUCCESS AND RICHES

1. Try to get into a business of your own, where you can use your fine intellect and discerning nature to sell the public on your products or services. The women make good as teachers, though their salaries are limited; Virgo women are not overly ambitious for fame and fortune and prefer the security of a position that pays a pension after twenty or more years of service. Virgo women are also good in cosmetology, interior decoration, and designing gowns or jewelry.

The Virgo man likes the business world and often goes into catering, restaurants, nightclubs, bars, and businesses that deal in foods and products related to the kitchen.

2. You may not be the type of Virgo that responds to labor, physical hard work, or dealing with practical, down-to-earth things like

food, running hotels, or other businesses catering to the public. You might easily become proficient as an accountant, in electronics, or computer work. Try to establish and expand your own small business and grow as you will do better there.

3. Slow but sure financial growth is the rule for you if born in Virgo. The speculations in stocks, gold, oil, or uranium are not for you, although many Virgos have been intrigued by these speculative ventures. You are better off in the safe and sure things, like buying a home or a piece of real estate that grows in value over the years.

4. You work well in conjunction with another person, and you might consider going into business with a friend or your marriage partner. Virgos do not like to make decisions or do things on their own without another person's reassurances. If you can go into a partnership with someone, you will be more successful than going it alone.

5. If you want to get rich quicker or become successful in whatever field you choose, try to overcome the tendency you have to be petty, detailed, and constantly looking for flaws. This is a negative trait that often bogs down many Virgos in the mire of vacillation, indecision, and pettiness and keeps them from adopting the broad viewpoint of overall success.

6. You make an excellent manager, director, or supervisor of other workers and you can achieve a degree of success in such activities, but here you must also be cautious not to let your superior mind become impatient with the slowness or lack of perception of the workers under you. You are a perfectionist and rapid in your thoughts and actions.

7. Learn to make friends of rich, successful, and socially prominent people by overcoming some of your shyness and reserve. Realize that very often it's not "what you know, but who you know" that counts. Join clubs of rich and successful people, and belong to groups of businessmen and women who can help you make contacts that can better your fortunes.

HOW TO MOTIVATE A LIBRA PERSON TO HELP YOU BECOME SUCCESSFUL AND RICH

When dealing with a typical Libra person, keep in mind the keynotes to his character: he likes peace and harmony in his relations with others; he is balanced mentally and does not like hysteria, confusion, and domination; he is born under the planet Venus that rules love and beauty; and he admires anyone or anything that brings out his love and admiration.

Libra is probably one of the most charming signs in the zodiac and you will find Libras friendly and approachable. They can be manipulated to buy your services or your products if you appeal to their desire to be well-groomed, to be beautiful, or handsome, and to have emotional security.

If you try to sell a Libra person a home, do not dwell on the central heating and air conditioning, but stress the beauty of the gardens, the peace and quiet and quality of the neighborhood, the location of schools, the feelings of security and comfort that will come by living in such a house and in such a superior neighborhood. Your Libras are inclined to be snobbish in social relations and will do anything to maintain a level of standards and ideals that they are accustomed to. They are honest, balanced, warm, and deeply emotional, and you can appeal to them by recognizing these superior qualities in their characters.

Libra rules the seventh house which deals with partnerships, and Libras enjoy working in close cooperation with others. You can go into such a partnership with the Libra-born and be sure they will be honest, industrious, and efficient. They are good at meeting the public and make excellent salesmen. If you do ally yourself with someone born in the sign of Libra, try to choose a business dealing with Venus products: cosmetics, smart clothes and women's attire, hair styling and cosmetology, or making and selling jewelry. These people can also go into interior decorating and become a big success.

To get some idea of the diversity of talents that Libras have, look at this list, and then realize that you are dealing with a highly intellectual, talented, and artistic type of person, and so you must make your approach on the mental and intellectual plane rather than the monetary or material side: writers Gore Vidal, Thomas Wolfe, Eugene O'Neill, Truman Capote, Arthur Miller, and Faith Baldwin; politicians and public servants Sam Yorty (former mayor of Los Angeles), James Farmer, William O. Douglas, Lester Maddox, Charles Percy, and Wayne Morse.

IF YOU WERE BORN IN LIBRA DO THESE THINGS TO WIN SUCCESS AND RICHES

1. Realize that you are the type that likes comforts and luxuries and the things money can buy. You will need money in large quantities to provide all the things you dream about, so make up your mind that you will concentrate on and give time to the accumulation of a fortune. As you spend money almost as fast as it comes in, and sometimes faster, you must get into something that brings in large sums of money quickly. As your sign is ruled by Venus which rules beauty, love, women, and women's products, try to find an outlet for your talents in some profession where you can capitalize on women. Cosmetology, owning your own beauty salon, and selling cosmetics, gowns for wealthy women, jewelry, and reducing salons are a few things that you could make big money in rather quickly. You are also very expert in interior decorating and might have your own business. Investments are not favored in stocks or speculative ventures.

2. You are also very clever in dealing with people socially. People like you; you are cheerful, smiling, witty, and a good conversationalist; you should try to join a social club attended by prominent people. Go to dances, parties, and social events to meet individuals who are important and rich. In no time at all you will have built a large group of leading socialites who will invite you to their homes and through whom you can enlarge your social and business contacts. If you are in a business providing some service which these people need, or a product they can buy from your company, it is obvious they will patronize you quicker than some stranger.

3. Try also to organize groups in the arts; a musical group that might make popular recordings could bring you a fortune from one recording. You are quick at discovering talent, and as a business manager or agent for such a talent, you could be a big success with very little effort on your part.

4. If you can go into partnership with some wealthy person who will back you in a business, you will have an ideal situation in which to use your talent and their money to get rich. One Libra woman I know runs a beautiful home in a very rich community where elderly people from wealthy homes retire to a kind of country-club environment. She is a charming hostess; people with

elderly parents who need care patronize her; and she is becoming rich.

5. A reducing salon or health spa is another very good way for Libra people to get rich quick. Catering to wealthy women who want beauty treatments, reducing diets, and exercises, you might associate yourself with a nurse or a doctor and open such a place where wealthy women would pay large sums for your services.

6. Typical Librans like to instruct others. If you have the talent for this, you might try opening a hobby school for adults, in which you provide instruction in ceramics, painting, sculpting, water coloring, and handicrafts. You will find that people are very responsive to a self-help adult school of this type, and you can arrange with neighborhood merchants to have exhibits of your students' products in their shops and attain publicity for your venture.

7. I know a Libra lady who studied artificial flower making and began to create beautiful bouquets which she sold or rented to restaurants, beauty salons, and other businesses for a monthly fee, with a change of bouquets each week. Soon she was training ten women in her home to make the flowers, and finally she was earning $50,000 a year through her artistic creations. You can study this art for a few weeks and see if you have talent in this direction before going into it.

8. Another excellent field for the Libra-born to make money in is catering to children. Have a doll shop, specializing in beautiful dolls of all types from every country, and you will soon build a very lucrative business that pays rich dividends.

Warning to Librans! When you do start the money flowing into your bank account, save a regular amount and put it into solid investments, such as real estate or expanding your business until you have real security; then begin to spend the excess cash you have accumulated.

HOW TO MOTIVATE A SCORPIO PERSON TO HELP YOU BECOME SUCCESSFUL AND RICH

When you are trying to influence a Scorpio person to bring you wealth and success, realize what type of person you are dealing with. There are two distinctly different types of Scorpios. One is the highly idealistic, aspiring, intellectual Scorpio, represented in astrology by the symbol of the soaring eagle. The other is the stinging scorpion lurking in the physical and material shoals of sensuality, selfishness, greed, and avarice.

The high type of Scorpio you can approach on an intellectual level, and the lower type of Scorpio you can reach through his physical and material interests. With the latter type, dwell on how much money your product or service will make for him, show him how he can improve his lot in life, make more money, become more socially prominent, raise his standards for his family and himself. Cater to his sensual nature and appeal to his love of food, sex, and power. These Scorpios are very much interested in putting on a show; they like recognition and acceptance. If he is the head of his department in a large organization and you are trying to sell him something, wine and dine him, have a pretty girl companion along to intrigue him, and you will undoubtedly get a contract from him or his company for your services or products.

You can appeal to the higher type of Scorpio on the basis of his interest in a beautiful home, his love of his family, and his loyalty to his children. He wants security in his finances; he wants to buy his own home and settle down; he likes to entertain his friends and serve the best wines and foods and liquors; he likes to show off a fine car and boast of a beautiful wife who wears the finest gowns and the best jewelry. He likes ostentation and would rather be seen in a very expensive Cadillac than in a Volkswagen, for he is NOT a gas saver or pennypincher. He spends lavishly on the things he likes and wants.

Cater to your Scorpio, high or low level, by recognizing his accomplishments; flatter his achievements and his appearance; tell him how you enjoy his company; laugh at his jokes; and admire his possessions. Scorpios are very lavish with their love and money when it comes to a person they like. They will help you achieve your goals if they are in high positions, they very often back people in businesses dealing with food, liquor, garages, transportation, medical or drug activities, and sports. You can seldom get a Scorpio to give you an outright gift of money to do with as you wish (there are always strings attached, such as a controlling interest in the business), but if you win their interest and promise them big returns on their money you may get them to finance you in a business of your own. Scorpios can make you rich if you can overcome their disadvantageous traits.

IF YOU WERE BORN IN SCORPIO DO THESE THINGS TO WIN SUCCESS AND RICHES

1. Study your own nature, your weaknesses, and strengths; find out which type of Scorpio you are, and then work to overcome some of the blatant weaknesses of the lower-natured Scorpios. These are extravagance and wastefulness, boastfulness, ego that is dominating and demanding, ostentation that often causes you to go into debt to drive a better car or live in a house you cannot afford, selfishness, sarcasm, cruelty, and lack of consideration for the feelings or rights of others.

Then work to overcome these negative traits and try to become the higher, more idealistic, and unselfish type of person represented by Scorpio when it rises to its highest potential.

2. Work on refining your personality, acculturating your mind, and developing your artistic and creative tastes for the finer life. Have a master scheme to achieve riches and success. Align yourself with a marriage partner and start a family of your own early in life, so you will have a high goal to work toward: the security of your family, the education of your children, the acquiring of material possessions that will bring you and your family comfort and luxury in the years ahead.

3. Remember that the Scorpio ruler is Mars, and this means action, combativeness, and aggression. Do not get into dull routine work where you are forced to sit at a desk eight hours a day. You need to get out, to meet people, to express your dynamic, magnetic personality. You can make a fortune in the selling and promoting of merchandise, in meeting the heads of big corporations, and selling your services or products.

4. You also have talent for engineering, transportation, television production or directing, as well as for the publishing fields and advertising. Once you get into any of these fields you will quickly rise to the top in your work and make a fortune.

5. Avoid being petty and pennypinching, as some Scorpios are, for you must realize that to make money you must spend money. For example, taking the head of a company out to dinner and to a nightclub can pay rich dividends in the future. Also advertise your products or services in order to capture the public attention. Scorpios often hate to spend on things that are intangible, but realize

that you are expecting to make money from the public so you must tell them about your wares.

6. Invest in stocks only if you have expert advice; many Scorpios want to make money quickly, so they jump into stocks on the advice of some friend and lose all their money. Scorpios have often made big money in the stock market, but only by knowing the field or having an expert advise them on investments.

7. More Scorpios grow wealthy through real estate investments, waiting for the long-term gain than through speculation in risky ventures. Buying income units and houses and redecorating them, or land for future development offer excellent future possibilities for growth and riches. Scorpio is not a sign that grows wealthy overnight; it is a sign that depends on slow and gradual gains and then cashing in on the accumulated property at the appropriate time.

Examine the list of people in chapter two under the section dealing with Scorpios and what professions they should choose for a more complete list of professions and occupations that are suited to the Scorpio-born.

HOW TO MOTIVATE A SAGITTARIUS PERSON TO HELP YOU BECOME SUCCESSFUL AND RICH

Sagittarians are easy people to motivate and influence. Ruled by the benevolent planet Jupiter, they like people, and are cheerful, optimistic, and agreeable. By catering to their honesty, integrity, and friendliness, you can get almost anything you want out of them.

If you have a product or service to offer those born in Sagittarius, remember they like quality and performance. They are honest people and expect a fair deal. If you misrepresent something to them and they find out about it, they are finished with you for life. Always tell the truth even if it may hurt a sale, and you will win their eternal loyalty and affection. They will then always return for future services from you.

Sagittarians are naturally social-minded, and you can best influence them to patronize you by meeting them through social groups. Join clubs and organizations where you can seek out those born in this fortunate sign and when you do meet a Sagittarian, remember that they do not like ostentation and affectation.

Be honest, sincere, and simple in your approach. Their predominant interests are business, politics, sports, animals, and children. They love outdoor activities and are happiest in the country, surrounded by natural beauty. They have an independent spirit and do not like to be hemmed in, so do not try to capture them and hold their interest for too long a time. Be casual in your approach to Sagittarians, and you can generally win them over to your way of thinking.

Check the list of Sagittarians in various professions in chapter two and see what famous people were born in this lucky sign; then use your good judgment as to how you would approach them.

IF YOU WERE BORN IN SAGITTARIUS DO THESE THINGS TO WIN SUCCESS AND RICHES

1. If possible seek out a profession where you can travel. Your nature likes to be on the go constantly and you would do well representing some big company by traveling a great deal. You could also succeed by owning or operating a travel agency. You are excellent in public work of any kind where you meet people, as your ruling planet, Jupiter, governs the public, government posts, finances, and investments in stocks and commodities. You are at your best in positions of public trust, and you make a dedicated public servant. Politics is a natural field for you, and you can go far in winning public office and holding it over the years. See the list of those who have held public office, all born in Sagittarius, and it will give you greater confidence in yourself: Shirley Chisholm, Ramsey Clark, Margaret Chase Smith, John V. Lindsay, Adam Clayton Powell, Fiorello LaGuardia, and Strom Thurmond.

2. Money is not always the goal of those born in Sagittarius. However, Sagittarians like comfort and security, and money as a means to an end will mean a good deal to you. You should make plans for long-haul gains rather than a quick success, and try to engage in work that will hold your interest and bring you satisfaction. You can build a fortune by carefully investing your savings, or you can take a plunge in a business of your own and probably make a big success, for you are good in selling products or services to the public. You are independent and do not like to

go into partnerships as a rule. However, if you find a person as honest and reliable as yourself, possibly another Sagittarian, you can be successful in such ventures.

Remember that two of the world's richest men were born in this fortunate sign of Sagittarius, J. Paul Getty, the oil billionaire, and Andrew Carnegie, the steel magnate.

3. As your sign also rules religion, philosophy, and the higher mind, you could go into religious work or an occupation connected with large charitable organizations, raising money for them or doing some philanthropic work. This might not bring you riches, but it would bring you great personal success and satisfaction, as your sign requires something more from life than just making money. Also, if you choose the ministry as a life work you will be a great success and be able to win followers to your religious beliefs.

4. Because your social nature is so very agreeable and outgoing, you should get into organizations early where you can make contacts with the most influential and successful men and women in your community. This can be a political or social club, a church organization, or one of the many service clubs, such as the Rotary, Kiwanis, or Lions clubs, which are in every community. In this way you will often meet those influential citizens who will give you the social and business boost which every Sagittarian needs if he is to achieve outstanding success in his chosen profession.

HOW TO MOTIVATE A CAPRICORN PERSON TO HELP YOU BECOME SUCCESSFUL AND RICH

Your Capricorn person is a very complicated and difficult person to manipulate. He is very set in his ways, almost to the point of stubbornness and you cannot push him or force him. But you can know his inherent traits and weaknesses and work on these to influence him to help you in your rise to fame and fortune.

In every herd of cattle there is always a "lead cow." This is the one that all the other cattle follow. You will find that Capricorns like to be the head of anything they are associated with. Even if you are a Leo and want to dominate and lead the way, you cannot do this with a Capricorn. You must cater to this dominant trait in your Capricorn or you will get nowhere with him.

In every social or business activity, you will find somewhere a typical Capricorn leader. They like recognition and power. If you can do things that cater to this natural, innate trait, you can literally lead your Capricorns to do anything you want them to do. They like praise and recognition of their work. They like to be appreciated, admired, and patted on the back. They are so often the underdog in life that when someone comes along who appreciates their hard efforts to succeed, they are deeply appreciative and will reward such a person with loyalty and long-lasting friendship. A noted Capricorn is Richard M. Nixon who seemingly retired from public office with the injunction to the newspapermen that they would no longer have him to kick around. Typical of a defeated Capricorn, however, he came back from defeat and won high office twice in a row, only to run into Watergate, another big setback, which caused him to resign from the presidency. Two other Capricorn presidents also knew defeats; they were Andrew Johnson and Woodrow Wilson.

Don't try to borrow money from a Capricorn person, but if you want him to invest in your project, tell him how it will add to his prestige and allow him to take a prominent place in the organization as an advisor or associate.

In trying to win a Capricorn's business, show him how your product or your services will help him become more powerful, more prominent, richer, and more socially influential. You can capture his interest in big schemes to bring him fame, fortune, and social prominence. They like to rule over an empire, and this grandiose idea must always be kept in mind in dealing with Capricorn people. Howard Hughes and Aristotle Onassis were both born in this money sign.

IF YOU WERE BORN IN CAPRICORN DO THESE THINGS TO WIN SUCCESS AND RICHES

1. Pick some high goal that seems impossible to achieve and then diligently plug away at your work with only that goal in mind. This is usually the motivation you require to reach the top of the ladder of success.

2. Try to get into work that deals with buying and selling property or some commodity that is on a big scale, like the development of

land to make a complete community, the building of a chain of grocery stores, automobile products, or selling machinery, cars, household appliances, television, and radio sets.

3. Try to get a bank loan and go into business for yourself as early as possible, for you operate best in an independent business where you are your own boss. Establish credit early in your career for you will require plenty of capital to carry out your big dreams in the future.

4. If you go into politics, try to make contacts with as many important people as possible. Always keep in mind the symbol for your sign, the goat climbing a mountain. It takes him lots of time, but by slow, surefooted, plodding methods, he gradually reaches the top. So, in like manner, work slowly but painstakingly, using your natural high intelligence, and you will achieve the top in any profession you choose. See the tenacity, endurance, and confidence of Mohammed Ali, the boxing champion, who would never admit defeat. He is typical of Capricorn. Prizefighter Floyd Patterson, another Capricorn, fought every known type of opposition and formidable opponents to win the championship. J. Edgar Hoover and Stalin were both born in Capricorn. Both held onto their hard-won positions for several decades or more. This is typical of the endurance possessed by your sign, so never give up.

5. One of the surest paths to certain success that many Capricorn people choose is the profession of law. This is one of the best fields for you, for from this you can go up the ladder of success in many different fields. Many criminal and civil attorneys were born in this sign, and they generally went on to higher posts in state, city, or federal government where they amassed fortunes.

HOW TO MOTIVATE AN AQUARIAN PERSON TO HELP YOU BECOME SUCCESSFUL AND RICH

Aquarians are noted for their benevolence and kindness in helping those who are unfortunate or underprivileged. This is an excellent sign to ask for favors if you keep in mind certain basic traits about these charming people.

You can get Aquarians to do things for you and help you in your climb to fame and fortune if you recognize their need for praise, flattery, and adulation. Never criticize or downgrade one born in this sign, for they are highly sensitive and will withdraw into a shell if you find fault with them. To get their full cooperation and approval, give them recognition for their sterling qualities and admire their achievements. If you have to stretch your imagination a little, do so, for it will pay you rich rewards with Aquarians.

Aquarius is one of the most intellectual signs in the zodiac, so your appeal to Aquarians must be on the mental plane rather than the physical. They are also highly idealistic and charming. (Aquarius is the most magnetic of all signs.) Cater to these traits, and if you are trying to sell them your goods or services, tell them how it will better them and their families, and thus help the world. Recognize their charm and magnetism and show them how riding in the car or living in the house you are trying to sell them will add to their social or business lives and make them more admired by friends and acquaintances.

Always try to appeal to the altruistic side of the Aquarius nature. They are "do-gooders," attempting to inspire, uplift, and educate the masses. Show them how you can help them achieve these objectives and you will win their support and admiration.

Keep in mind the following men born in this great sign: Abraham Lincoln, Franklin D. Roosevelt, and Thomas A. Edison, and you will have a fairly good idea of the qualities they possess and how you must handle them to obtain benefits or assistance from them.

IF YOU WERE BORN IN AQUARIUS DO THESE THINGS TO WIN SUCCESS AND RICHES

1. Curb some of your restlessness and time-wasting by setting your goals for the future, then set to work to make them come true. You are inclined to lose interest in things quickly, and you often try one thing after another, losing valuable time in your climb to success.

2. Select key people in social and business circles that you can appeal to in your efforts to achieve certain goals. Remember you have a very valuable commodity to sell—yourself. Your strong personal magnetism and charm can win over the support and assistance of high-placed people. Get into social, political, and business circles where you can meet such important people and then use

them in your climb to fame and fortune. See how Aquarian Ronald Reagan became governor of California, using powerful friends and people who could help him in his ambitions. From being an ordinary actor he has used his Aquarius charm and magnetism to become a serious future contender for the White House.
3. Realize that you are better at being a business executive or head of an organization than you are at being an ordinary worker. Try to use your head rather than your hands to achieve success and riches. Working for others will never get you rich for you always manage to spend more than your salary. Money must come in large quantities to satisfy your voracious appetite for luxury, comfort, and high living.
4. You are excellent in the investment or insurance fields where you can be around big money. In insurance, you should strive for an executive position, rather than a job as a salesman. In the stock and bond business you can use your charm and compelling magnetism to get rich clients to buy any stock you suggest. This field is ideally suited to you for quick growth and riches. However, a word of caution about gambling—do not try to get rich by speculative means. It is all right for you to be in the stock-selling business, as long as you do not buy stocks that are purely speculative. Generally, Aquarians lose money when they try to speculate in anything but real estate.
5. Get into any of the typical new age professions for quick riches and success. This is the Aquarian age, and all the modern marvels of television, aviation, spaceships, computers, radio, motion pictures, and electronics in general are under the influence of the planet Uranus which is your ruler. Anything original or different intrigues you. Charles Lindbergh was an Aquarian, and in the early days of aviation he made his voyage over the Atlantic which brought him fame and fortune because of these very traits we are talking about. You will notice that most Aquarians are in the forefront of their profession. Evangeline Adams, an Aquarian, was in the forefront of the field of astrology in the early days when it was struggling for recognition. James Joyce, the noted writer, is recognized for his unique style. Norman Mailer won recognition with his original and vivid stories of the war. James Michener, another Aquarian, is also noted for the style and distinction of his writing. Gertrude Stein, famous writer of the early twenties, was original and provocative with her typically Aquarius literary talent. Get

into any field where this wonderful originality and advanced thinking can bring you immediate notice and recognition from the public. It will pay you rich rewards.

6. You might get into the publishing and writing fields if you were born in Aquarius. You have a powerful imagination and could make your mark in the fields of fantasy and imagination. Lewis Carroll and Charles Dickens were Aquarians. Try your hand at writing original TV or motion picture scripts, or books dealing with the strange, weird, and unusual, and you can easily win outstanding fame and riches.

HOW TO MOTIVATE PISCEANS TO HELP YOU BECOME SUCCESSFUL AND RICH

First, learn what Pisces people are really like, so you will better understand them and how to manipulate them to do your bidding.

There are two types of Pisceans as represented by the two fish, one swimming upstream, the other downstream. The drifter, the inconstant Piscean, is the one that swims downstream in life, without purpose or direction. He is usually a weak and vacillating person, and it is best to avoid him. He is often afflicted with a drinking or gambling problem, and he may wind up a miserable failure, dependent on others for his sustenance.

The Pisces you want to attach yourself to, and whose aid you want to enlist, is the one that is on the upward path to success and riches. You can get assistance from this type of Piscean easily, for he is generally easygoing, kindhearted, and always trying to help others. In fact, that is often a weakness in even the strong Pisceans.

Appeal to your Pisces through the emotions, not through reasoning and rationality. His children, his wife, his pets, his friends all mean a great deal to Pisceans, and by talking about them, or showing an interest in their welfare, you can not only capture the Piscean's attention, but win his wholehearted support. He will buy your products or take your services if you can assure him that they will help him give more and be more to those closest to him emotionally. Your Piscean lives for his family and friends. He likes a beautiful home so he can entertain his friends. He enjoys a beautiful car, not for himself, but so he can share it with those close to him. Always use this approach when trying to motivate Pisceans.

Pisceans are also very sociable and you can meet them easily at parties or the homes of friends. They are usually very sympathetic toward those who are struggling to achieve success and will voluntarily help their friends and acquaintances. They are the most agreeable people in the zodiac, and you can easily win their assistance in your endeavors.

See the list of Pisceans given in chapter two, and you will realize that some of the world's most talented and wonderful people were born in this great sign.

IF YOU WERE BORN IN PISCES DO THESE THINGS TO WIN SUCCESS AND RICHES

1. Overcome the strange duality of your sign by making up your mind to be firm, strong, and surmount your wavering and vacillation. Choose a career or course in life and then try to adhere to it, changing only when forced to do so by outer circumstances over which you have no control. By cultivating firmness of purpose and determination, you will reach the top more readily in whatever profession or vocation you choose.

2. You have a very strong magnetism for people and can easily go into sales promotion work and make a fortune. You have hypnotic powers, and by using your eyes and commanding others with your mind, you can easily win their support and make them buy your products or services. Get into real estate, insurance, investments in stocks, or other financial fields where you can influence others to invest their money and you will make a fortune.

3. The healing arts are also excellent for a Piscean to try in his bid for fame and fortune. The women make excellent nurses, but to become rich, you should go into running and operating a convalescent home or a home for aged and retired rich people. Also Pisceans are often highly successful in medicine, chiropractic, and pharmacy.

4. As you have a fondness for food and good living, you could make your fortune in running a restaurant or catering service. You are a natural party giver and might be good as a hostess or arranger of social events over which you preside.

5. One of the outstanding fields at which Pisceans, both men and women, excel is cosmetology. You could own and operate beauty salons that cater to a fashionable clientele and become extremely successful.

6. You must learn to hold onto your money as one of the Piscean traits is generosity, and you might easily spend all you make on helping indigent friends or members of your family.

6

How to Use Astrology to Make You a Social Success

One of the world's best-sellers of all time was a book called *How to Win Friends and Influence People* written by Dale Carnegie. This showed the concern most people have about achieving social success, having the right friends, and being able to live with their friends and coworkers in peace and harmony.

Certainly, by knowing what people like and do not like, you can have a perfect key to their characters. Astrology can give you this guidance to popularity, friendship, and greater social success. Your friends can make or break you; it is vitally important that you understand how to appeal to those born in various signs of the zodiac. When you are dealing with an Aries, for example, you use a totally different approach than that required when trying to win and hold the friendship of a Piscean. You can be compatible with any sign of the zodiac if you observe a few "dos" and "don'ts."

In using the following information, find out the birthdate of the person you are trying to win or influence. As everyone is interested in astrology today and it is one of the main topics of social conversation in almost every group, it does not seem peculiar when you ask someone his birthdate. With that date known, you can proceed to shape your speech and actions in a manner that will have a direct influence on the new acquaintance you are trying to win or influence.

HOW TO WIN AND HOLD
THE FRIENDSHIP OF ARIANS

1. Do let them have their own way. Let them decide on the play you'll see the evening you go out together, the restaurant you'll dine at, and the seats you'll occupy. Make them feel their judgment is best and you are happy to follow their directions. Do this even if you're a Leo and it kills your ego to let someone else be first.
2. Do let them take the lead in conversation and don't interrupt when they're telling a funny story and let them know you've heard it before. They'll never forgive or forget.
3. Do give in to them if an argument arises about the latest scandal in politics. They think they know best and they know it all. You will win them forever if you can let them be the big brains of the party.
4. Do avoid tangling horns with them if you are a Taurus or a Capricorn, the bull and the goat, for Aries the ram will butt its way through all your opposition and win anyway.
5. Do let them boast and show off their intellect, and tell about their children's cute habits and their conquests in business and finances. Listen carefully and say, "You are great" and "I think you're wonderful!" in your conversations with Arians.

OBSERVE THE FOLLOWING
DON'TS WITH ARIANS

1. Don't ever try to force an Arian to your way of thinking but gently lead him, making him feel it was his idea all along.
2. Don't say things that arouse their tempers for they flare up quickly, but cool off as quickly. However, to win their friendship keep the sharp edges out of your conversation.
3. Don't wait for them to pick up the check, but reach for it quickly, and you will win them forever. Aries is not the most generous sign in the world.
4. Don't keep an Aries waiting, but show up on time, keep your word to him, and be lavish in your praise and appreciation of his punctuality, fairness, and sense of justice.
5. Don't criticize your new Aries friend or point out his defects;

HOW TO USE ASTROLOGY TO MAKE YOU A SOCIAL SUCCESS 97

he usually has many, but he doesn't like to hear about them. Pour on the flattery with a shovel, and don't be afraid he will see through you. This is his one blind spot; your Aries friend loves himself and expects everyone else will, too.

HOW TO WIN AND HOLD
THE FRIENDSHIP OF TAUREANS

1. Do be sympathetic and kind to Taureans, giving them consideration and attention. They are eager to be friendly and will respond with friendship when you show an interest in them.
2. Do expect them to be good conversationalists and give them a chance to respond to your comments. They do not like conversation monopolizers and soon cool toward such persons.
3. Do talk about the three things that interest Taureans most: money, food, and sex.
4. Do try to be witty and tell funny stories for your Taurean enjoys a good laugh and does not take himself as seriously as your pompous Capricorns or self-centered Leos.
5. Do admire their cars, homes, jewelry, children, or pets, as they like recognition of their possessions and respond with warmth and affection when praised.

OBSERVE THE FOLLOWING
DON'TS WITH TAUREANS

1. Don't argue with Taureans or try to push them in your direction as they are set in their ways and may resist you. Win them with logic to your way of thinking.
2. Don't intrude on their privacy by asking too many questions about their private lives. If you wait, they will soon open up and tell you all they want you to know.
3. Don't ask a Taurean to lend you money or do you a favor until you know him very well as he resents "pushy" people.
4. Don't ask them to be weekend guests at your home until you are very well acquainted with them.
5. Don't be impatient with Taureans for they are slow, take a long time to make a decision, and are inclined to resent people who try to rush them into anything.

HOW TO WIN AND HOLD
THE FRIENDSHIP OF GEMINIS

1. Do give them credit for having high intellectual powers and appeal to them on the basis of their superior intelligence.
2. Do talk about the modern scene in politics, art, music, literature, and current shows on TV as your Gemini is up to date on everything going on in the world.
3. Do appeal to his funnybone for Geminis are great wits, storytellers, and humorists. Dorothy Parker was a typical Gemini.
4. Do invite them to parties and social events, as they love meeting people and are charming guests as well as hosts. Elsa Maxwell, the famous party giver for celebrities, was a Gemini.
5. Do be diplomatic and subtle with your new Gemini friends; they have few rough edges and will admire you if you show polish, refinement of manners, and charm. President John F. Kennedy was typical of the Gemini charm and diplomacy.
6. Do remember that a Gemini person is a mental twin, sometimes a triplet.

OBSERVE THE FOLLOWING
DON'TS WITH GEMINIS

1. Don't try to outsmart them or show your superiority.
2. Don't adopt a critical attitude toward Geminis.
3. Don't show fits of temper or impatience with them.
4. Don't maintain a heavy atmosphere of gloom or moodiness; they love laughter. Bob Hope is a typical Gemini.
5. Don't get on boring subjects with Geminis.
6. Don't be shocked at their Jekyll and Hyde personalities.

HOW TO WIN AND HOLD
THE FRIENDSHIP OF CANCERIANS

1. Do be reserved and cautious when you first meet your new Cancer friend. He is apt to be wary and somewhat aloof until you know him better, and then he will show his true nature.
2. Do show an interest in the home, marriage, children, and domestic matters, as he is vitally interested in these things.
3. Admire your new Cancer friend and show him that you

appreciate his accomplishments. He is apt to have an inferiority complex and you can appeal to him with this attitude.
4. Do be the leader in conversation with your Cancerian for they are modest and sometimes shy, and they admire people who are leaders. President Gerald R. Ford is typical of Cancer.
5. Talk about art, music, and books with Cancerians, as they have high intellects and are very creative.

OBSERVE THE FOLLOWING DON'TS WITH CANCERIANS

1. Don't expect them to rush headlong into any new venture.
2. Don't disparage his accomplishments, his home, or his friends.
3. Don't be critical, impatient, or unsympathetic with him.
4. Don't ignore his need for love and sympathy.
5. Don't be impatient with his periods of moodiness and depression.

HOW TO WIN AND HOLD THE FRIENDSHIP OF LEOS

1. Do recognize his superior qualities and admit that he is the leader in everything you do together.
2. Do show great affection and admiration for your Leo friend.
3. Do flatter him and let him know you admire him tremendously.
4. Do give in to him when he disagrees with you.
5. Do let him tell about his grandiose plans and do admire them.
6. Do remember that Leo is the sign of the lion, king of the jungle, and let him roar to show his superiority and greatness.

OBSERVE THE FOLLOWING DON'TS WITH LEOS

1. Don't expect them to cater to you and your interests.
2. Don't look for them to spend money on entertaining you.
3. Don't forget that Leo, more than even Aries, must be number one.
4. Don't ignore their accomplishments; instead praise them lavishly.
5. Don't forget they love money, power, and social position.

Jacqueline Kennedy Onassis is a typical Leo; she loves the spotlight, power, and social prestige that she has achieved.

HOW TO WIN AND HOLD THE FRIENDSHIP OF VIRGOS

1. Do recognize their reserve and dignity and avoid prying into their private lives. Greta Garbo, of "I want to be alone" fame, is a Virgo.
2. Do show an interest in the latest diet, health, reducing fads, and foods in general.
3. Do talk about intellectual and mental interests also for remember Virgo is ruled by Mercury, planet of the mind.
4. Do be interested in music, art, and books and discuss these.
5. Do be careful not to flatter them too openly as they are very sharp and detect insincerity quickly.
6. Do recognize that they are the teachers of the zodiac, so let them correct your mistakes in grammar, straighten your tie, and even tell you how to arrange the furniture in your living room.

OBSERVE THE FOLLOWING DON'TS WITH VIRGOS

1. Don't try to appeal to their emotions; appeal to their intellect.
2. Don't show curiosity about their love lives or their sense of privacy as they resent this highly.
3. Don't criticize them and point out their defects.
4. Don't come on strong with flattery as they see through this.
5. Don't forget Virgo minds work like computers; they are cold and logical and seldom operate on emotions alone.

HOW TO WIN AND HOLD THE FRIENDSHIP OF LIBRAS

1. Do remember that Libra is ruled by sensitive Venus, so respect their fine sensibilities.
2. Do respect their sense of balance and harmony and try to keep within the limits of proper and moral conversation.
3. Do appreciate their romantic natures and talk about love, marriage, children, and the home when you meet them.

4. Do discuss social justice and elevation of the masses, remembering that Eleanor Roosevelt was a Libra.
5. Do avoid irritating Libras with too much detail and exacting information about any subject. They are easily bored.
6. Do understand their frequent use of wit and sarcasm to cover their sensitivity. It is a defense mechanism and not intended to harm others.

OBSERVE THE FOLLOWING DON'TS WITH LIBRAS

1. Don't direct or command Libras as they are set in their ways.
2. Don't criticize their personalities, clothes, or way of life.
3. Don't show coarseness, vulgarity, or commonness in your speech with them.
4. Don't upset their emotional balance by changing your mind too often.
5. Don't ignore their love of peace, beauty, poetry, and music.

HOW TO WIN AND HOLD THE FRIENDSHIP OF SCORPIOS

1. Do recognize that Scorpio people have strong wills and are dominant personalities. Let them take the lead in your new friendship.
2. Do appreciate their qualities of loyalty and friendship.
3. Do encourage their ambitious natures and their desire to rise to positions of power and success. Senator Robert Kennedy was a Scorpio.
4. Do know that they are interested in making money and having a life of luxury and ease. Talk about money and business.
5. Do tell your Scorpio friend often what a good sport he is, and show your admiration and respect for his talents.
6. Do avoid crossing him or making him angry at you, for he can become a formidable enemy and will seek revenge.

OBSERVE THE FOLLOWING DON'TS WITH SCORPIOS

1. Don't clash with Scorpio friends; you will live to regret it!
2. Don't deceive them or lie to them, for they like honesty.

3. Don't try to dominate them for they like to be the leaders.
4. Don't get caught up in their intrigues unless you like confusion and friction. They are past masters at this art.
5. Don't expect them to spend money on you or entertain you lavishly as they are often pennypinching.

HOW TO WIN AND HOLD THE FRIENDSHIP OF SAGITTARIANS

1. Do be open and aboveboard with Sagittarians as they like honesty and frankness above all.
2. Do respect their love of freedom and independence.
3. Do meet them halfway on everything as they are fair-minded.
4. Do show an interest in animals, sports, and outdoor activities.
5. Do discuss travel to foreign countries and international life.
6. Do appreciate their idealism, their intellects, and their scrupulous honesty.

OBSERVE THE FOLLOWING DON'TS WITH SAGITTARIANS

1. Don't mislead or misrepresent things to Sagittarians.
2. Don't impose your opinions or your will on them.
3. Don't be too intimate on first meeting as they are reserved.
4. Don't be immodest or talk openly about sexual matters.
5. Don't forget they are highly idealistic and intellectual.
6. Don't discuss money, your possessions, or work until you know them better.

HOW TO WIN AND HOLD THE FRIENDSHIP OF CAPRICORNS

1. Do recognize them as being mentally and intellectually superior.
2. Do let them lead you in conversation or social affairs.
3. Do praise them and appreciate their desire to succeed.
4. Do overlook their desire for privacy and being alone a lot.
5. Do forgive them for their seeming ruthlessness and coldness.
6. Do understand their love of power and achievement and the fact that they never give up.
7. Do cater to their desire for financial independence and security

and talk a good deal about honor, achievement, and overcoming adversity.

OBSERVE THE FOLLOWING
DON'TS WITH CAPRICORNS

1. Don't step on their toes or oppose them openly. They make unforgiving and formidable enemies.
2. Don't go back on your word with Capricorns.
3. Don't try to dominate them or impose your opinions on them.
4. Don't discourage them in their ambitions to rise to positions of fame, riches, and power.
5. Don't be surprised at their seeming indifference and coldness, but win their confidence first and they will become loyal and devoted friends.

HOW TO WIN AND HOLD
THE FRIENDSHIP OF AQUARIANS

1. Do respect their privacy and individuality.
2. Do admire their originality and intellectual superiority.
3. Do talk about brotherhood, peace, prosperity, and social justice. Abraham Lincoln was an Aquarian and so was Franklin D. Roosevelt.
4. Do tell them that more people in the Hall of Fame were born in Aquarius than in any other sign. They will admire your astuteness.
5. Do let them take center stage often and tell of their conquests, exploits, and great deeds.
6. Do praise their brilliant minds and let them know you are a satellite, orbiting in the gravity pull of their charm, magnetism, and greatness.
7. Do express your love and admiration of them and show them affection, forgiveness, and adulation.

OBSERVE THE FOLLOWING
DON'TS WITH AQUARIANS

1. Don't expect them to show undying loyalty for you as they often judge people on the basis of what they can do for them, not on their merits or true qualities.

2. Don't try to capture their love or friendship but be satisfied to be on the outer periphery of their affections.
3. Don't expect them to live by the ordinary rules of social and personal behavior; they make their own rules and often break them.
4. Don't judge, criticize, or blame them for their defects. Theirs is a divine mission in life, so they believe, and no one must interfere with it. Kaiser Wilhelm was Aquarius; so was General Douglas A. MacArthur.

HOW TO WIN AND HOLD THE FRIENDSHIP OF PISCEANS

1. Do recognize their sensitivity and reserve and do nothing to shock or discourage them when you first meet them.
2. Do show admiration, love, and affection for Pisceans as they respond to warmth and friendliness.
3. Do honestly admire their traits of kindness and their desire to help the unfortunate and downfallen.
4. Do appeal to their high idealism and sense of beauty.
5. Do praise them for their kindness to others and for their humane and self-sacrificing natures.
6. Do recognize their highly spiritual natures and the fact that they are striving to overcome their faults and weaknesses.

OBSERVE THE FOLLOWING DON'TS WITH PISCEANS

1. Don't be upset at their human failings; if they are the type of Pisces that vacillates, remember that their symbol is two fish, one swimming upstream, the other downstream.
2. Don't put your burdens and problems on their frail shoulders.
3. Don't become involved in their financial problems or borrow money from them.
4. Don't try to force your Piscean to do what you want; appeal to his emotions, not to his reason or intellect.
5. Don't forget the Pisces character is like a child; he is deeply appreciative of anything you do for him and never forgets a friend who has been good to him.

7

How Your Stars Affect Your Health and Length of Life

Each sign of the zodiac is said to rule a particular section of the body and the various vital organs. If you learn the various tendencies to illness and work to avoid them, you can often escape many of your sign's worst afflictions and add to your life energy and length of life.

By all means, if you should need medical advice, seek out a physician who can help you. Astrological indications are not meant to supersede the advice of medical experts, but you may be helped in understanding your weaknesses as well as your strengths through this study and avoid some of the common ailments that afflict humanity.

HEALTH INDICATIONS FOR THOSE BORN IN ARIES

Your sign is said to rule the head, the brain, and the parts that make up the head, such as the eyes, ears, and nose.

The Aries-born are apt to suffer from colds in the head, sinus infections, and disturbances to the eyes and ears when the planets are under adverse aspects. Mars, the ruling planet of Aries, also subjects Aries children to fevers, infections, and afflictions of those areas in childhood. If the children are properly inoculated by a competent physician in the first year of life, they can avoid many of these disturbances.

As this sign also rules the brain, they must be cautious not to overwork and not to live under pressures, fears, worries, and anxieties that might cause mental disturbances and nervous breakdowns.

For better health and longer life, the Aries-born should strive to maintain a balance in their lives between the mental and physical activities. They should work hard but rest a great deal and sleep a full eight hours at night to get them over nervous tension and emotional exhaustion. As they are perpetual dynamos of creative activity, they need plenty of fresh air, exercise, and relaxation to counterbalance this constant flow of mental and physical energy in their strenuous lives.

They should eat plenty of energy-producing foods, such as carbohydrates and sugars, balanced by meat proteins, vegetables, and fresh fruits in season.

HEALTH INDICATIONS FOR THOSE BORN IN TAURUS

Your sign is generally a strong one with built-in stamina, endurance, and vitality. You can endure much in the way of stress and strain which seldom breaks you down mentally as it does your more sensitive Aries brothers, but you have other weaknesses.

Taurus itself rules the throat area and we often find that Taureans are afflicted with a variety of throat problems from swollen and infected tonsils to diphtheria to quinsy and throat abscesses. As this area also rules the voice box and vocal chords, we often find Taureans afflicted with hoarseness, nodes on their vocal chords, and laryngitis. Bing Crosby, a typical Taurean, is said to owe his success to this tendency of having nodes on his vocal chords which gave his voice the soft, velvety, and throaty quality that won him fame and fortune.

Taureans often fall prey to virus infections which start in the throat and mouth area and spread to the lungs. They are frequently victims of allergies and germ infections from infected sinuses or tonsils.

But perhaps the most frequent cause of illness for Taureans is connected with their tendency to overeat and to gain weight when they reach forty years of age, sometimes earlier. This tendency often leads to high blood pressure and heart trouble and causes early death through apoplexy and heart disease.

Taurus can live out its normal life span by controlling the appetites and avoiding oversmoking and overdrinking as they grow older. They should also get plenty of rest and exercise.

HEALTH INDICATIONS FOR THOSE BORN IN GEMINI

Gemini people are ruled by the planet Mercury which gives them very active minds and bodies and predisposes them to overwork, restlessness, and anxiety.

Gemini itself is said to rule the chest area and the lungs and the organs in the area. Geminis often have trouble with the gall bladder, and require surgery to correct it; this is due to their highly sensitive natures and their reaction to emotional problems which often interfere with their metabolism. This, in turn, affects digestion and creates inflammation of the gall bladder.

But the most frequent complaints from Gemini-born are chest colds, a tendency to bronchitis, comsumption, and asthma. If they smoke excessively, they frequently are in danger of heart trouble and lung cancer.

Many of the diseases suffered by Geminis are psychosomatic in nature. Their highly fanciful and nervous minds often imagine symptoms and create illnesses which are of an emotional origin rather than physical in nature. They also suffer frequently from hypochondria, imagining ills they do not possess. They may develop brain fever or inflammation of the membranes of the brain owing to their excitable natures, their constant restlessness, and their tendency to worry excessively.

They can avoid many of their illnesses by avoiding extremes of cold and heat, by adopting a more leisurely pace of living, and by having periodic checkups with their doctors to be sure they are not developing real illnesses. They often live to be eighty-five to ninety if they take good care of themselves.

HEALTH INDICATIONS FOR THOSE BORN IN CANCER

Cancer-born are highly sensitive people and their sign rules the stomach and digestive organs. There is no relationship whatever with this sign and the disease that bears the name cancer. I have checked up on this and find that people born in Cancer do not have this dread disease more than those born in other signs, so do not let this become an anxiety.

Realizing the sensitivity of Cancerians, we can readily understand why so many of them have trouble with their digestive organs. As nervous tension often produces difficulties in the stomach, these people must try to avoid excessive worry, fear, anxiety, and moodiness. The first John D. Rockefeller, a Cancerian, is said to have had an artificial stomach as a result of an operation that removed part of his intestines. No doubt he was affected by nervous tension engendered by his efforts to build the multimillion-dollar fortune which he left his heirs. But don't forget, he lived to be nearly a hundred.

Those born in this sensitive sign must watch their diets carefully as most of their difficulties arise from overeating meat, starches, and carbohydrates. They must avoid acidosis and other complaints related to an unbalanced and overrich diet.

HEALTH INDICATIONS FOR THOSE BORN IN LEO

Leos are fortunate in almost everything they undertake and generally have good fortune in health matters. Born under the rulership of the sun when it is high in the heavens in midsummer, Leo people seem to be able to survive occasional bouts of illness, and to have the energy and vitality capable of sustaining them throughout their long, productive lives.

This sign is said to rule the loins and the back, and the Leo-born often have to be careful of these areas of the body. They are also subject to lumbago and occasional nerve inflammation of the limbs, such as sciatica.

Leo people should adopt a health regime which includes sun-baths and hydrotherapy, in which they immerse themselves in hot water baths and relax, letting their entire nervous system recover from the day's tensions and anxieties. They should avoid over-medication, as their systems are very sensitive to drugs of all kinds; they should use only those that are recommended by their physicians in times of pain or distress and not try self-medication.

Many Leo people are prone to be indolent and not exercise sufficiently, thus growing obese as they grow older. They must watch their diets carefully and eat plenty of the green, leafy vegetables that are heavy in minerals and vitamins from the sun. They should avoid overeating bread, all carbohydrates, and sugars, and go heavy on fruits and natural grains.

HEALTH INDICATIONS FOR THOSE BORN IN VIRGO

Virgo is considered the strongest of all signs in the zodiac outside of Leo and Capricorn. This earth sign is strong and durable and Virgos often live to be eighty-five to ninety with great ease. They are very much concerned about health and diet and rarely let themselves become overweight; they seldom have diseases associated with dietary mistakes.

However, there is a weakness in the Virgo system as there seems to be in all the signs of the zodiac. This sign is said to rule the bowels and lower intestines. They have to be very careful not to overeat roughage that might irritate the colon and produce inflammation of that area. They often suffer from colitis, spasms, dysentery, and chronic constipation.

The Virgo diet has to be carefully supervised, maintaining a balance between meats, vegetables, and fruits, with special emphasis on natural, unprocessed foods. The Virgo-born seem to have sensitive stomachs and cannot tolerate overprocessed foods. They should strive to eat whole grains and natural foods. They benefit from yogurt, honey, and sugars that come naturally through dates, figs, and fruits.

Virgos need plenty of sleep and rest as this sign rules the nervous system. They often suffer from insomnia and cannot drink too much coffee, and they must be careful of excesses in smoking or the ingestion of alcoholic beverages. They usually live long because their delicate digestive system requires care in diet.

HEALTH INDICATIONS FOR THOSE BORN IN LIBRA

The sign of Libra rules the kidneys and the bladder. Seldom are the Libra-born sick; they are surprisingly healthy. But when they are careless and eat too much meat or imbibe too much alcohol, they are likely to have difficulties with the liver and the kidneys.

Libra people are apt to have occasional pains in the back region, where the kidneys are located, and sometimes require treatment or therapy with diathermy and heat applications. Very often a sensitive Libra person will have ulcers due to nerves, and sometimes Libras will experience nervous reaction in the colon and digestive tract. Some develop Bright's disease or spinal trouble. Also these sensitive people often have diabetes or its opposite disorder, hypoglycemia, which is the secretion of too much insulin in the bloodstream, making them very tense, nervous, and irritable.

Libra people should not overeat at any one meal but should eat several times a day in small quantities that will not overload their systems. They should regularly flush out the lower colon and bowels to avoid constipation.

HEALTH INDICATIONS FOR THOSE BORN IN SCORPIO

If you were born in Scorpio you are subject to certain disorders which might be avoided if you are forewarned.

Scorpio rules the reproductive tract and the organs connected thereto. Many women born in this sign have difficulties during and after childbirth. Occasionally they have ovarian cysts and fibroid tumors, but these are generally benign.

The alimentary canal and the rectal region are often involved in Scorpios, giving them a tendency to piles, hemorrhoids, and fistulas which often require medical and operative care.

Scorpio people also have to be careful of blood infections due to venereal diseases, and must use caution and avoid unhygienic conditions in their personal grooming and in bathrooms. They are also subject to blood poisoning. There is also a liability to kidney stones and similar complaints, owing to faulty diet, overdrinking, and indulging in other negative habits such as excessive smoking.

As Mars is the ruling planet of this sign, we often find Scorpios developing fevers and high temperatures. Children born in this sign often exhibit such symptoms early in life and must be watched carefully.

HOW YOUR STARS AFFECT YOUR HEALTH AND LENGTH OF LIFE 111

HEALTH INDICATIONS FOR THOSE BORN IN SAGITTARIUS

Sagittarius is one of the luckier signs in respect to health and long life. Jupiter, your ruling planet, generally favors you with dynamic good health, vitality, and energy that incline you to a long life of useful activity.

This sign is said to rule the thighs and buttocks and sometimes these may become affected. However, this area of the body is seldom actually involved with health problems for those born in this sign.

The sign is inclined to rich living, including overeating of meats and sweets which can give Sagittarians such afflictions as blood disorders, gout, tumors, and fevers. As a rule Sagittarians have health disturbances in the early years suffering from the usual childhood disorders; then when they mature they seldom have many severe illnesses.

If you are careful and observe strict dietary rules, you can avoid most of the diseases others are subject to. For instance, most Sagittarians like the healthy, outdoor life; they exercise regularly, often indulging in active sports, and this has a tendency to keep them healthy and free of disease.

However, if Sagittarians indulge in excessive smoking or drinking, nightclub activity until late hours, and do not get sufficient rest, their vitality becomes lowered and they are then easy prey to infectious disorders and germ invasion of the bloodstream. A normal diet, plenty of rest and exercise, and moderate living habits assure Sagittarians of living a long life and one free of disease.

HEALTH INDICATIONS FOR THOSE BORN IN CAPRICORN

Capricorn is said to rule the knees and this part of the body often shows signs of weakness. Sometimes Capricorn people fall and injure this part of the legs. However, being surefooted, most Capricorns are able to avert this type of disorder.

There are other weaknesses in the Capricorn body which tend toward certain disorders and diseases. Capricorns are subject to rheumatism and arthritis, disorders in the joints of the body, and accumulations of calcium deposits which may not cripple them but often cause pain and discomfort. The Capricorn system is sensitive to irritating foods and should avoid hot mustard, peppers, chili sauce, and condiments, as well as sodium chloride (table salt) which may be an irritant causing inflammation in the joints and other disturbances.

Capricorn people are also subject to severe colds, influenza, and virus infections if they are not cautious and if they let their resistance become lowered by overwork, stress, and strain. Another ailment that sometimes afflicts Capricorns is eczema and other forms of skin disorders. They must strive to keep the skin clean, bathing often and avoiding contact with people having such skin diseases.

Capricorns have great longevity, and with normal caution can easily live into the eighties. Their ruling planet Saturn favors people who survive past fifty and sixty years of age, giving them long life and vitality that carry them easily into advanced old age.

HEALTH INDICATIONS FOR THOSE BORN IN AQUARIUS

The sign of Aquarius is surprisingly free of illness and infection. Uranus, the ruling planet of this sign, seems to endow Aquarians with remarkable recuperative powers. They have a tendency to nervous exhaustion, insomnia, and overwork which can be avoided. As this sign is a highly nervous one, Aquarians are subject to nervous breakdowns more than those born under other signs of the zodiac.

The typical Aquarian has his share of childhood disorders, but if the parents take advantage of medical science and inoculate their children against the common childhood ailments, many of these disorders can be avoided. Parents should be especially careful to vaccinate against polio as this often strikes those born in Aquarius. President Franklin D. Roosevelt was an example of an Aquarian who suffered from polio as there was no vaccine in his time.

As Aquarius rules the nervous system and often gives rise to strokes and brain tumors, Aquarians should avoid prolonged periods of mental stress and relax and rest frequently during the day. They are often very athletic in early youth but become more inclined to sedentary habits as they mature and their muscles and tissues become flaccid and subject to accumulations of fat. This can lead to high blood pressure and heart disease. Franklin D. Roosevelt died of a stroke of apoplexy due to the tensions he had as a wartime president.

HEALTH INDICATIONS FOR THOSE BORN IN PISCES

The sign of Pisces is said to rule the feet, and these people often suffer from fallen arches, bunions and corns, and a general weakness in that area of the body.

By avoiding standing on their feet for too long a time, Pisceans can sometimes escape these problems. They are also subject to varicose veins which are not harmful but may prove distressing from an aesthetic viewpoint.

Another frequent affliction of Pisceans is gout. This may be prevented by eating a balanced diet, and avoiding too much red-blooded meat, and eating more fish and poultry.

Pisceans are highly sensitive, moody, and depressed, and often have periods of deep melancholy and anxiety. They may require psychiatric or psychological counseling to help dispel the gloom and morbidity that hound these sensitive people.

Another disorder that Pisceans must watch out for is blood infection that might lead to blood poisoning. They should immediately take care of any skin cuts that might admit bacteria, and avoid contamination from insecticides, pollutants, and harmful drugs.

As Pisces is the twelfth sign of the zodiac, called the house of self-undoing, these people are often addicted to sleeping pills or other forms of drugs and sometimes become alcoholics. Of course, this opens up a field of disorders that have nothing to do with their sign, but which are due to their personal weaknesses. They should avoid drugs except under their physician's direction.

8

For Women Only: Things You Should Know About Male Friends, Husbands, and Lovers

According to members of the women's liberation movement, there is very little difference between men and women. As someone remarked, "Thank God for that little difference!"

Actually, according to the astrological signs there is a great deal of difference in the characteristics of men and women born under the same sign. It is vitally important for you, a woman, to know how to respond to men born in the different signs of the zodiac.

We shall here study the various signs of the zodiac from a woman's viewpoint and appraise their potentials as friends, husbands, and lovers. If you are already married and find he is not born in a compatible sign to yourself, do not despair and rush for the divorce courts; study your husband's sign as revealed below, and find out how you can still make a go of a marriage that is floundering or seems to be on the rocks.

If you are interested in winning a male friend or lover, find out his birthdate and get the key to his character. You can then use the information given here to plan a winning campaign that will give you power over him and the ability to sway him in your direction. Learn his likes and dislikes; find out the type of woman he secretly admires; discover his sexual strengths and weaknesses, and then you are better equipped to handle your man and lead him to the marriage altar.

THINGS YOU CAN DO TO WIN AND HOLD AN ARIES MAN

1. Realize that although Aries is one of the most intellectual signs in the zodiac, your appeal to an Arian should not be through the intellect alone. He likes fun and frivolity and believes in extramarital sex. You will have to use your own judgment on that score, but you'd better know his full sex potentials before marrying your Aries man. As someone remarked, "Divorces start in the bedroom."
2. Let him have his own way and don't try to boss him.
3. Let him take the lead in conversation and in choosing restaurants, theaters, and other places to go.
4. Give him plenty of praise and admiration.
5. Tell him often what a great guy he is and how you admire his intelligence, his efficiency, and his wit.
6. Laugh at his jokes and make him feel ten feet tall.
7. Tell him how you love the home, children, and cooking.
8. Show him you love the simple life and advise him not to spend too much money.
9. Never discuss marriage plans, but let him take the lead.
10. Do not show jealousy or possessiveness, at least not until after marriage. Aries does not like possessive women.
11. Show an interest in golf, tennis, swimming, and sports.

Some famous Aries men are J. William Fulbright, Edmund Muskie, Harold Stassen, John D. Rockefeller, 3d, Robert F. Wagner, William Holden, Thornton Wilder, Eugene McCarthy, Thomas Dewey, Wernher Von Braun (father of our space age), and Charlie Chaplin.

THINGS YOU CAN DO TO WIN AND HOLD A TAURUS MAN

1. The men born in this sign are ruled by Venus, the planet of love and beauty. They admire beauty in a woman, and you should strive to always show your best and most charming side to a Taurean.
2. Realize that he is a romantic soul, despite his seemingly sensual and physical nature, and let him express his romantic nature.
3. Win Taurus with kindness, love, and food as he is very responsive to these three forces.

4. Talk about his business, his interests, and his hobbies.
5. Go to parties, dances, and social events with your Taurean.
6. Admire his talents, but don't flatter him unless you mean it.
7. Give him little gifts to show your admiration and love.
8. Avoid trying to dominate him as he likes to be boss.
9. Try to overlook his jealousy and fits of temper as he soon gets over them and becomes docile and manageable again.
10. Realize that Taurus men make good husbands, providers, lovers, and fathers, but do not push them into marriage; let them take the lead as they do not like aggressive women.

Some famous Taurus men are Bing Crosby, Dean Martin, Pat Boone, Jacob Javits, Joe Louis, Archibald MacLeish, Willie Mays, Winthrop Rockefeller, Philip Wylie, Archbishop Fulton J. Sheen, Ronald Ziegler, Dr. Benjamin Spock, and Harry Truman.

THINGS YOU CAN DO TO WIN AND HOLD A GEMINI MAN

1. Gemini men are more mental and intellectual than Taurus men, so you can go heavy on conversation that is deep, philosophical, and worldwide in its interests.
2. Show an interest in art, music, and the latest books.
3. Do not be disappointed if he does not sweep you off your feet romantically. He is not overly passionate like your Taurean and he must be really interested first.
4. Give him more rope than you do other signs for he resents being held too firmly to any orthodox course of action.
5. Admire his intellect, his reserve, his sophistication.
6. Share his sense of humor as he likes witty conversation.
7. Don't tell him what to do, whom to see, or what to eat.
8. Be there when he needs you, without intruding on his privacy.
9. Realize that he is a dual personality, and do not be hurt when he seems to be cool and indifferent towards you.
10. Take occasional short trips with him on weekends for he is restless, easily bored, and requires frequent changes of scenery and action.

Some famous Gemini men are Joe Namath, Dr. Norman Vincent Peale, Wilbur Mills, David Rockefeller, William Scranton, Hubert H. Humphrey, and Robert S. McNamara.

THINGS YOU CAN DO TO WIN AND HOLD A CANCER MAN

1. Cancer men are charming, gentle, kind, and loving; avoid hurting their feelings and respond with understanding and sympathy to their lovemaking and advances.
2. Show an interest in his family, his relatives, and his home.
3. Let him know you are a typical homebody who loves children.
4. Get him into romantic moods by using soft lights, perfumes, soft music, and romantic dialogue.
5. Show your Cancer man you know how to run a home, cook good food, and care for a future family.
6. Admire his business ability and praise his efforts to win success in his field.
7. Take an interest in politics and international affairs.
8. Build a solid social life with him as he likes people.
9. Don't criticize him or find fault with him as he is very sensitive to criticism. Wait until after marriage for this.

Some famous Cancer men are President Gerald R. Ford, John Glenn, Mark O. Hatfield, Henry Cabot Lodge, George McGovern, Nelson A. Rockefeller, Leo Durocher, and Jack Dempsey.

THINGS YOU CAN DO TO WIN AND HOLD A LEO MAN

1. Leo is the sign that rules the fifth house having to do with love affairs and children. Leo men are in love with love and you must respond with love and idealism to their romantic natures.
2. Recognize that they are self-centered and cater to them.
3. Give your Leo man plenty of praise and flattery.
4. Tell him often what a great lover he is and how you love him.
5. Talk about his high goals and ambitions for future success.
6. Take him on a busy round of parties, dances, and social events as he is very sociable and enjoys being around people.
7. Don't tell Leo men your problems or worries as they enjoy being around people who are carefree and happy.
8. Let him know he is the boss and that you are a willing follower.
9. Avoid arguments and discussions on religion and politics.
10. Don't try to change him, as he is set in his habits and ways.

Some famous Leo men are Arthur Goldberg, Henry Ford, Ben Hogan, George Meany, Ogden Nash, Casey Stengel, and Whitney Young.

THINGS YOU CAN DO TO WIN AND HOLD A VIRGO MAN

1. Admire their superior intellect and brain power.
2. Show that you are practical, down to earth, and a realist.
3. Disregard their criticisms and faultfinding as they are perfectionists and nothing is ever quite right for them.
4. Talk about health foods, the latest diet fads, and weight control as they are fascinated by these things.
5. Respect their sense of privacy and don't intrude on it.
6. Try to keep up to date on the latest books, plays, art, music, and world affairs as their minds are interested in these things.
7. Try not to be bored by his too smug personality and show him that you admire him for his reserve, tact, and diplomacy.
8. Take an interest in sports and outdoor activities.
9. Don't talk about money or ask how much he makes.
10. If he proposes marriage don't stall and put it off as he quickly cools if rejected in love.

Some famous Virgo men are Alfred G. Vanderbilt, Lyndon B. Johnson, Warren Burger, Lewis B. Hershey, Walter Lippmann, Melvin Laird, Arnold Palmer, George Wallace, and Roy Wilkins.

THINGS YOU CAN DO TO WIN AND HOLD A LIBRA MAN

1. Realize that Libra men are romantic, flirtatious, and inclined to fall in love easily. Show interest, be very feminine and romantic, but pretend he's the only man in the world as far as you're concerned.
2. Let him see you always dressed in your best; use makeup discreetly.
3. Appeal to his high idealism and snobbishness.
4. Cultivate conversational sparkle, wit, and humor; but avoid criticism, sarcasm, and ironic wit.
5. Be interested in social reform and helping unfortunates, remembering that Eleanor Roosevelt and Gandhi were Librans.

6. Tell your Libra man often that he is a genius. He will believe you wholeheartedly and think you are very perceptive.
7. Avoid emotional tantrums, fits of temper, and hysteria as his delicate balance is easily upset by emotionalism.
8. Let him know you think marriage is wonderful and that you are prepared to dedicate your life to him and his needs.

Some famous Libra men are Gore Vidal, Mickey Mantle, Arthur Schlesinger, Jr., William O. Douglas, James Farmer, Truman Capote, Arthur Miller, Senator Charles Percy. Three past presidents of the United States born in Libra were Chester A. Arthur, Zachary Taylor, and Rutherford B. Hayes.

THINGS YOU CAN DO TO WIN AND HOLD A SCORPIO MAN

1. Scorpio is known as the sex sign; this especially applies to men, so make the most of this and give them the sex appeal they fully expect.
2. Avoid trying to dominate your Scorpio man but let him be the leader in love and other activities.
3. Don't oppose Scorpios openly; they have quick tempers, and are apt to overreact to opposition. Use sweetness and kindness and, of course, sex to get power over your Scorpio man.
4. Although Scorpio men love freedom, they will settle down and marry if you assure them you want children. They like children and usually make good husbands and fathers when they do marry.
5. Recognize his ambitious nature, his desire to become rich and successful.
6. Put the soft pedal on spending as he may be tight with money.
7. Try to ignore his stinging sarcasm and satirical wit, or react with well-barbed quips and a quick laugh.
8. Be lavish in your praise of his talents and flatter him a good deal as he likes to be told he is great.
9. Let him take the lead in most things as he thinks he knows best in choosing places to eat, what theater to go to, and other social activities.

Some famous Scorpio men are Senator Robert Kennedy, Richard Burton, Billy Graham, Spiro Agnew, W. Averell Harriman, Sargent Shriver, Jonas Salk, and Will Rogers. Four presidents born in

Scorpio were James Garfield, James Polk, Theodore Roosevelt, and Warren G. Harding.

THINGS YOU CAN DO TO WIN AND HOLD A SAGITTARIUS MAN

1. Your Sagittarius man loves his freedom and independence; make believe you will give him plenty of rope after marriage.
2. Cater to his idealism, superiority, and good nature as he likes admiration and recognition of his fine points.
3. Show him loyalty and affection as he admires these qualities in his sweetheart and wife.
4. His mind is deep and serious; talk about philosophy, show an interest in ESP and comparative religions, and travel with him.
5. Become an ardent lover of animals: dogs, cats, and horses.
6. Try to cheer him up when he has his frequent moods and depressions.
7. You probably met him through a social event, not in business, so take him to parties, dances, and social events.
8. He admires women who believe in women's liberation, so play up your love of freedom and independence. Do not be a shrinking violet with your Sagittarius lover.
9. As he is a sports enthusiast, share in his love of the outdoors, forcing yourself to enjoy swimming, tennis, golf, and football.
10. Talk about serious things: the stock market, business, money, big investments in real estate, land development, and property.

Some famous Sagittarius men are John V. Lindsay, oil billionaire J. Paul Getty, Noel Coward, William Buckley, Jr., Sir Winston Churchill, Ramsey Clark, Joe DiMaggio, and James Thurber.

THINGS YOU CAN DO TO WIN AND HOLD A CAPRICORN MAN

1. Respect his desire for secrecy and privacy in his personal life and do not intrude in that sphere until you know him well.
2. Overlook his seeming emotional coldness as he is warm and responsive when he is in love.
3. Admire his tenacity and determination, and let him know you believe in his ambitions to achieve fame, power, and riches. (Re-

member some very rich people were born in this sign, including Howard Hughes and Aristotle Onassis.)
4. Be there when he needs you to console him in his moments of defeat and disaster; Capricorns have plenty of these.
5. Maintain a dignified and poised presence when you go out with your Capricorn lover or husband.
6. Dress in the latest fashions, but in a subdued way, and do not go to extremes in hairdos, color schemes, or wear freakish costumes as Capricorn is very conservative and correct.
7. Don't drag him to concerts, operas, or openings of art galleries.
8. Let him have nights out with the boys frequently as he feels at home with male companions.
9. Don't arouse his anger or try to make him jealous.

Some famous Capricorn men are Barry M. Goldwater, J. Edgar Hoover, Stalin, Floyd Patterson, Mohammed Ali, James Baldwin, J. D. Salinger, and James Farmer. Four presidents of the United States were Capricorns—more than any other sign in the zodiac.

THINGS YOU CAN DO TO WIN AND HOLD AN AQUARIUS MAN

1. You're aiming high when you set your sights on an Aquarius man. More of them are in the Hall of Fame than those born under any other sign in the zodiac. Be prepared for many headaches and heartaches if you want to win and hold your Aquarius man.
2. He admires brainy women, so be conversant on many subjects.
3. Share in his humor and biting wit as he likes to josh people and play practical jokes on his friends.
4. Be willing to take a backseat in the magic circle of his magnetism and charm and don't expect to dominate him.
5. Try to be elegant, fashionable, socially aware, and let him know you have your mind set on high goals for him to achieve.
6. Overlook his petty tantrums when he can't have his own way.
7. Remember that he is a passionate lover, but his ardor can cool quickly.
8. Take an interest in electronics, politics, aviation, and the fields of music, art, and literature as topics of conversation.
9. Play hard to get at first as Aquarians want what they can't have.

Famous Aquarius men are Charles Lindbergh, General Omar

Bradley, Louis Nizer, S. J. Perelman, Norman Mailer, Ronald Reagan, James Michener, Paul Newman, Norman Rockwell, and Hank Aaron.

THINGS YOU CAN DO TO WIN AND HOLD A PISCES MAN

1. Realize that your Pisces man is a dual personality and try to understand why he goes in two directions at the same time.
2. He is a very emotional man; appeal to him through the emotions, not the intellect.
3. Give your Pisces man plenty of love, sympathy, and understanding.
4. If he has some bad habit, such as drinking, gambling, or smoking, don't try to break him of it as he will resent you.
5. Cater to his sentimental nature, and let him know you are aware of his desire to help people and of his unselfishness.
6. Create a peaceful and serene environment where he can be at ease with you.
7. Dress in frilly, colorful costumes, go in for theatricals, emphasize your makeup, and be a clinging-vine type of woman.
8. Recognize his deep spiritual nature and his need of faith.
9. He is generous with his money, but don't urge him to spend too much as he admires people who can save for a rainy day.
10. He is apt to have many problems with people he has helped who turn against him; try to sympathize with him when he needs it.
11. He is very sexually oriented and likes constant adoration.

Some famous Pisces men are John B. Connally, Mike Mansfield, Edward M. Kennedy, David Sarnoff, Robert Lowell, Mickey Spillane, William L. Shirer, Earl Warren, and David Dubinsky.

9

For Men Only: Things You Should Know About Female Friends, Sweethearts, and Wives

Astrology can point out the various traits and characteristics of the women in your life and show you how you can become a better friend, lover, and husband.

Women are *not* all alike. Erase this erroneous concept at once. If you want to get the most out of your relationships with women, whether that relationship is romantic, social, or business, know them according to the signs under which they were born. This will help remove much of the mystery about women.

The twelve signs of the zodiac produce twelve distinctly different types of women, from the cold, almost frigid type to the warm, emotional, and responsive type. You can pick a clinging-vine, helpless type of girl if you are a typical Aries, bristling with masculinity, virility, and the desire to protect your woman from the world. Or, if you are a cool, ambitious would-be millionaire Capricorn, you must certainly know that there are two signs in the zodiac that would help you rise to fame and fortune and at the same time give you plenty of love and affection.

But whatever sign you were born in, check this list of the various types of women born in the twelve signs of the zodiac, and choose the one that you feel would be most suitable as a sweetheart, friend, or wife. For the most compatible signs in love and marriage, study chapter three of this book.

THINGS YOU CAN DO TO WIN AND HOLD AN ARIES WOMAN

1. Do not try to clip their wings and restrict them in their ambitions to become independent and successful. Career first, home and babies second; this is the usual Arian idea of life.
2. Cater to their sense of leadership; even though a woman, an Arian likes to lead. Let her choose the restaurant when you dine out; let her suggest the theater you'll go to; let her be the one to pick the car, the home, the furnishings you'll buy.
3. Aries women are passionate, affectionate, and responsive. Give her plenty of love and you can hold her interest forever.
4. Do not expect her to be the best housekeeper in the world; she expects the man she marries will be rich enough to afford a maid.
5. Give your Aries woman plenty of laughs; she is the life of the party, so don't try to make a drudge of her.
6. Your Aries girl is somewhat of a flirt, but don't let this throw you. However, don't let her catch you flirting or two-timing her as she has a violent temper and will create a scene.
7. Share an Aries woman's interests; if you love sports and expect her to give her life over to sports, you will be very disappointed. She will do what she wants to do and you'd better learn to like it.
8. Your Aries woman is brainy and intellectual. You must match her intelligence or she'll quickly tire of you.
9. She will be energetic, active, and a dynamo of power; you will have to learn to keep up with her many activities, so get plenty of rest.
10. She likes to spend money and expects you to make it, so you will be spurred on to greater success by your Aries woman, but you might also be spurred on to bankruptcy.

Some famous Aries women are Gloria Swanson, Bette Davis, Joan Crawford, Clare Boothe Luce, and Mary Pickford.

THINGS YOU CAN DO TO WIN AND HOLD A TAURUS WOMAN

1. Court your Taurus woman with gentility, love, and kindness.
2. Always be a gentleman, courteous and considerate as she is a Venus child and is sensitive, loving, and beautiful.
3. Talk about music, art, good books, and social activities.

4. She loves the home and children; let her know you do, too.
5. Give your Taurus woman little gifts frequently: a box of candy, a few flowers, an inexpensive piece of costume jewelry as her Venus nature makes her sentimental and romantic.
6. She will probably be typical of Taurus in that she loves music, singing, and dancing. Share in her artistic interests.
7. If she is impatient and shows a bit of jealousy frequently, disregard this and be even more patient with her and loving.
8. Show affection for her mother and father for she is usually very close to members of her family.
9. Show her that you are eager to start a home and rear a family as she is devoted to the home and loves children.
10. Cater to her good business judgment and ask her advice about investments and your career. She will love talking about these things.

Some famous Taurus women are Queen Elizabeth II of England, Carol Burnett, Kate Smith, and Shirley Temple.

THINGS YOU CAN DO TO WIN AND HOLD A GEMINI WOMAN

1. Realize that your Gemini woman is the most fascinating of the entire zodiac, but the most difficult to win and hold. You will be puzzled at her duality and may not understand her. She is intrigued by mystery and change, so be a little aloof and do not rush her with romantic suggestions, but wait until your acquaintanceship deepens before becoming too amorous.
2. Your Gemini woman is charming, witty, and sparkling with a great sense of humor, but also biting sarcasm, so do not be hurt by her sharp barbs. Learn to be amused at them.
3. This sign is ruled by Mercury, the mental planet, so your Gemini woman is smart, up to date, conversationally adept, and she expects you to keep up with her rapid pace both physically and mentally.
4. She is restless and likes to take many trips; frequently suggest weekend visits to mountain resorts or the seaside.
5. She can be very moody and depressed when her twin projects the pessimistic side of her dual nature; try to be sympathetic and understanding when she has these moods.
6. Your Gemini woman is so talented that she may put you in the

shade when it comes to business; let her have her career and try not to show jealousy or put women down as being inferior to men.
7. She will enjoy going to parties and dances, so take her out frequently and don't expect her to be a homebody.
8. Try to be understanding when she is half an hour late for she will always have a plausible excuse.
9. She aspires to high places and admires people who are educated, cultured, and socially oriented. Cater to this trait, and let her know you are studying to improve yourself culturally.
10. She may be studying music, painting, or something artistic; don't make the mistake of telling her her singing is terrible, or her art atrocious. She can turn against you quickly for this.

Some famous Gemini women are Isadora Duncan, the Duchess of Windsor, Elsa Maxwell, and Judy Garland.

THINGS YOU CAN DO TO WIN AND HOLD A CANCER WOMAN

1. Cancer women are practical and yet idealistic. They are ruled by the moon and are highly imaginative, romantic, and loving. Respect their extreme sensitivity and don't rush them into anything.
2. They love children and the home and are eager to marry early and have a family. Let them know at once you are a family man and you will have won half the battle.
3. They are interested in money, business, and success, so discuss your business plans with them and let them know that your aims are high.
4. Sensitive Cancer is also often moody and depressed. Learn to take these moon cycles with poise and calm; they soon pass.
5. Be prepared to take on a mother-in-law if you plan a future with a Cancer woman. The mother is often very close to her.
6. Cancer women like social activities but they are not gadabouts, so do not rush them into big social activities as you would a Gemini. They enjoy small, intimate groups in the home rather than nightclubs and big social activities.
7. At times Cancer women are silent and seem withdrawn; do not intrude on these contemplative periods.
8. They often want three or four children, so gear yourself for a big family, a big house, and big expenses if you marry a charming Cancer woman.

9. A Cancer woman is highly conservative and careful; if you are a gambler or like to risk money in the stock market, she will most likely discourage you as she likes security and buying a home and land for future growth.

Some famous Cancer women are Barbara Stanwyck, Lena Horne, Anne Morrow Lindbergh, and Pearl S. Buck.

THINGS YOU CAN DO TO WIN AND HOLD A LEO WOMAN

1. Women born in the sign of Leo are among the most charming and beautiful of all women. Be prepared to take a seat in the shade if you marry one as her scintillating and magnetic personality makes her always number one.
2. Leo women love beautiful clothes, expensive jewelry, the best run and the most beautiful home on the block, the most exclusive car, and a husband who is brilliant, successful, and socially prominent. If you can fill the bill, Leo is for you.
3. Try to understand her dominant and aggressive personality, and don't object if she chooses your suits, your hairstyle, and the food you are to eat.
4. If you want to become successful and rich, marry a Leo woman for she has the power to push you to the top.
5. Try to keep up a cheerful and optimistic facade as Leo women are cheerful, buoyant, and natural optimists.
6. You will never have quarrels or friction with your Leo woman if you can let her have her own way in everything. If you oppose her she will pout and sulk, but will get over it. If you oppose her too often, you will soon find yourself in the divorce courts and paying big alimony. She will manage all this with a smile.
7. Leo is called the royal sign in the zodiac; treat your Leo woman like a queen and let her rule the home, your social life, and your business as well as your finances.

Some famous Leo women are Clara Bow, Jacqueline Kennedy Onassis, Lucille Ball, and Edna Ferber.

THINGS YOU CAN DO TO WIN AND HOLD A VIRGO WOMAN

1. Your Virgo will be a practical and realistic person who is easy to get along with. Don't make rash promises to her, but keep your

word, be on time, and give her plenty of intellectual stimulation.
2. Once you get to know Virgo you will find she is soft, feminine, and warm, but she puts on a cold, aloof, and reserved facade to keep people from intruding. Take it slow and easy in trying to win her love and admiration.
3. Disregard her tendency to correct your grammar or point out your personality defects; she is a natural-born teacher and cannot help it.
4. Don't be fooled by the saying in astrology of "Virgo, the virgin." Your Virgo woman is very sex-oriented and not hard to please in that department, but she may be somewhat aggressive, so curb your distaste for aggressive women if you want to win her love.
5. Virgo women like the home, food, and the kitchen; even if they are career women, these things come first, so marry her and know she will be a good companion, housewife, and mother for your children.
6. She is a quiet person when you first meet her, shy and reserved in society, but when she knows someone she warms up. Take her to small, intimate groups for dinners or parties and avoid the spotlight or large crowds with your Virgo woman.
7. She will like music, art, and literature, so try to get on an intellectual plane with her when you first meet. Let love and sex come later when she gets to know you better.

Some famous Virgo women are Claudette Colbert, Lauren Bacall, and Greta Garbo.

THINGS YOU CAN DO TO WIN AND HOLD A LIBRA WOMAN

1. If you love a Libra woman you have selected a natural for she is ruled by Venus, the planet of love and beauty. She is generally beautiful in features and in form and loves fine clothes, beautiful jewelry, and a charming home environment. Promise her the moon, and then try to give it to her, and you will win her heart forever.
2. She is somewhat of a flirt as she is in love with love, and likes to test her powers over men's hearts; do not be jealous of her, but try to understand her nature.
3. Be romantic with her, court her with gallantry and charm; recite

beautiful poetry and have plenty of soft music when she is in a romantic mood (ballads and sentimental waltzes, not rock and roll).
4. She is sensitive and does not like quarrels or friction, so avoid arguments and never raise your voice.
5. Take her to plenty of parties and social events for she is a natural social butterfly and likes people.
6. She is highly moral and idealistic and does not like cheap, shabby environments or affairs. Promise her marriage, and you can win her love.
7. She is interested in social reform and helping the underdog, so be sympathetic to such causes as women's liberation and social justice.

Some famous Libra women are Lillian Gish, Carole Lombard, Helen Hayes, Janet Gaynor, and Faith Baldwin.

THINGS YOU CAN DO TO WIN AND HOLD A SCORPIO WOMAN

1. Scorpio women are very attractive sexually and are highly emotional and romantic. You can win them by admiring their beauty and charm and appealing to their sense of loyalty and devotion.
2. Don't try to dominate your Scorpio woman; she will listen to reason and logic but cannot bear to be told what to do.
3. Use flattery carefully for she detects falsity and resents it.
4. Try not to incur her anger or sarcasm as these are very cutting when she is antagonized.
5. There are two types of Scorpio, the eagle and the scorpion. Try to find out which she is. Treat her with kid gloves if she is the sensual, sarcastic, and venomous Scorpio. If she is the eagle, you can trust her and have confidence she will be a good wife and mother.
6. She is high-minded and ambitious for her lover or husband, so aim high; try to let her guide and inspire you to your goal.
7. The Scorpio woman likes to spend money, if it is someone else's. She loves luxurious gifts, like diamonds and fur coats, so be generous with her if you can afford it.

Some famous Scorpio women are Queen Marie Antoinette of France, Hedy Lamarr, Vivien Leigh, Katherine Hepburn, and poetess Marianne Moore.

THINGS YOU CAN DO TO WIN
AND HOLD A SAGITTARIUS WOMAN

1. You have chosen one of the finest signs of the zodiac; appreciate her honesty and loyalty and don't ever betray it.
2. Your Sagittarius woman is kind, generous, honorable, and loving. Give her plenty of love and affection, and show her you appreciate her qualities.
3. Don't ever try to deceive her or cheat on her; she is not apt to forgive or forget easily, as she expects undying loyalty.
4. Give her a feeling of freedom in her marriage; don't ask her where she was or whom she saw when she was out.
5. She will inspire you to become a big success for she likes accomplishment and achieving worldly recognition.
6. She is apt to want to be a career woman but still have a family of her own and a well-run house. Try to go along with her career aspirations.
7. She is a rational, reasonable woman and you can talk over problems without hysteria or anger. She is calm and cool in crises.
8. Make her your true partner and buddy, share in her love of outdoor sports and animals, and go on frequent trips with her.

Some famous Sagittarius women are Margaret Chase Smith Irene Dunne, Mary Martin, and Shirley Chisholm.

THINGS YOU CAN DO TO WIN
AND HOLD A CAPRICORN WOMAN

1. Capricorn women can be charming and responsive once you know them well, but they are apt to seem formidable and cool at first. Don't let this fool you, but warm them up with lots of attention, flattery, and little gifts. They are really sentimental at heart and warm up to people who recognize their good qualities.
2. Realize that Capricorn people love power and position; build this angle in your relationship with her, and let her know you want to become someone big and important.
3. Don't try to force your Capricorn woman to do anything; appeal to her logic and reason instead, and she will comply.
4. Show her you can save money and be provident; she admires people who can save for a rainy day.
5. She is apt to be moody and depressed very often and has a very

serious side to her personality; try to cheer her up, make her laugh, and take her to dances and parties often.

6. Capricorn women are proud of beautiful, well-organized homes. She wants to marry a man who can furnish a magnificent background for her social and personal life.

7. Don't ask her to have four or five children; she likes a small family, not more than two. If you want a brood get a Cancer or Taurus woman.

Two famous Capricorn women are Marlene Dietrich and Ethel Merman.

THINGS YOU CAN DO TO WIN AND HOLD AN AQUARIUS WOMAN

1. Aquarians are usually charming, mysterious, and beautiful. You will fall under their magnetic spell quickly, but don't give in too easily or they will lose interest in you.

2. Talk about the theater, latest TV shows, books, art and music, and intellectual subjects with your Aquarius woman.

3. She likes admiration and flattery, so be lavish in this respect.

4. You may feel left out of her magic circle at times as she is apt to be rather fickle, flirtatious, and changeable.

5. She is highly intelligent and you can appeal to her reason and logic rather than to her emotions.

6. Your Aquarius woman is also very intuitive. Don't try to lie to her about your relations with other women; she will know that you are lying.

7. If you reject her or betray her she can be very venomous and vindictive, so be careful in this regard.

8. Your Aquarius woman is apt to marry more than once; they are the most often-married sign in the zodiac, so be careful not to get involved unless you can handle such a highly volatile and independent woman.

Some famous Aquarius women are Zsa Zsa Gabor, Eva Gabor, Lana Turner, famous astrologer Evangeline Adams, Mrs. Harry Truman, and Margaret Truman.

THINGS YOU CAN DO TO WIN AND HOLD A PISCES WOMAN

1. Your Pisces woman is a very sensitive and beautiful person who responds to love, gentility, and kindness, so use these qualities in winning her love and attention.
2. She is apt to be sympathetic toward unfortunate people, so be careful she does not involve you in her charitable acts.
3. She will enjoy a beautiful home and children which she prefers to a career. Give her a quiet, peaceful environment.
4. She is likely to be somewhat of a visionary and highly idealistic; avoid being harsh and too realistic with her.
5. She may be somewhat indolent and not overly ambitious in her desire to become a success. She is better in the home than in having a career, so offer her marriage and motherhood.
6. She likes financial security for the future, so show you are a good businessman and able to handle money.
7. Pisces women like parties, social life, theater, art, music, and good books; they enjoy an evening out but generally prefer their own homes and close family ties.
8. Pisces women are passionate and responsive in love, but keep sex on a refined basis and don't be crude, rough, or harsh.

Some famous Pisces women are Jean Harlow, Elizabeth Taylor, Edna St. Vincent Millay, Elizabeth Barrett Browning, Ellen Terry, and Lillie Langtry.

10

How Your Stars Can Bring You Peace of Mind, Joy, and Fulfillment

Each sign of the zodiac has been endowed with certain traits and characteristics that especially fit those born in it for a definite place in the scheme of things. When you are aware of your own path to achievement, you can implement the positive forces at work in your stellar influences and subdue the negative ones. You can then achieve the peace, tranquillity, and fulfillment that each person should ultimately attract for his destiny.

HOW ARIES PEOPLE CAN FIND PEACE, JOY, AND FULFILLMENT

The fiery, restless Arian is often unable to find peace and happiness. The fault lies in the fact that you are apt to be too aggressive and eager for achievement. You must win your high goals in life, make your big fortune, buy the fine home, and have the best car. There are no in-betweens for you.

There is nothing wrong with being ambitious and wanting the best in life, but try to be happy and find satisfaction in the many wonderful experiences of your life that you will have as you struggle to reach the top of the ladder of success.

Learn to enjoy simple everyday things that you can share with your friends and acquaintances.

Relax more often and don't go such a rapid pace. Don't be afraid to go to sleep for fear of missing something.

Work at your job eight hours a day; then leave it at your place of business and enjoy your family, your friends, and have periods of time when you forget all about your ambitions to succeed.

Fall in love early if you want to be joyous and fulfilled. Marry, have a family of at least two children, and you will begin to have a purpose for living as well as a motivation for greater success.

Act and feel like a millionaire as you work towards your goal. Go to an occasional play, a fine restaurant, a plush nightclub, and feel expansive, rich, and successful.

Curb your impatience, harness your temper, and find enjoyment with your friends as you often shatter your peace of mind and happiness by your own irritable nature.

HOW TAURUS PEOPLE CAN FIND PEACE, JOY, AND FULFILLMENT

You have a very good start on the upward path to peace, joy, and fulfillment. Being born in the rather fortunate sign of Taurus and ruled by the planet of peace, beauty, and love, Venus, you are able to enjoy most of life's thrilling moments.

To add to this natural proclivity to joy, learn to make more of your social life. You are apt to be friendly, but you are somewhat reserved and aloof when it comes to meeting people. Make it a point to expand your acquaintances with people, meet new friends, and increase your attendance at parties, dances, and interesting social events.

Don't put yourself in a dull routine of business, making money, and paying bills, but vary the monotony occasionally. Do something new, break the old habits of seeing the same people, going to the same places, living at the same place, visiting the same vacation resort. Taurus people are inclined to become dull from doing too much of the same thing too often.

Have a five-year plan in which you work toward achieving some new goals: learn a new language; prepare yourself for travel to foreign countries you will one day visit by studying their history and cultures; take up a hobby of music, singing, photography, painting, or some sport you thoroughly enjoy.

Look the field over in love before you decide to marry your childhood friend. You may discover there is someone else more nearly suited to your romantic temperament.

Learn to add to your practical, conservative nature another

dimension of intellect and creativity by studying the lives of great musicians, artists, authors, inventors, scientists, explorers, and industrialists. This will add zest to your own life.

HOW GEMINI PEOPLE CAN FIND PEACE, JOY, AND FULFILLMENT

You especially need to give time and attention to building a more peaceful mind and a happier destiny. You are pulled in too many directions at the same time and this is apt to cause confusion and emotional disturbances.

Try to merge the two natures that your Gemini sign has given you. This is a talented sign but a restless and often an unhappy one. Make a decision about your right work, your suitable romantic partner, your social activities, and then try to stick to your decisions in these matters.

On the surface, you are a happy, fun-loving person. But like all clowns, when the music stops, the dance ends, and the guests have gone, you are likely to have tears on your pillow. Even a typical Gemini funster like Bob Hope has a really deep, serious streak in him, and undoubtedly he has these moments of loneliness and feelings of inadequacy. Try to fill your life with more substantial values; find something you can do to help others, such as working with charitable organizations; build interests in other people and community activities; and you will take your mind off your own problems and your limitations.

Try to be a more sincere and loyal friend and people will seek you out and give you their friendship.

To be peaceful and have greater joy, you must learn how to curb your indecision and vacillation. Study psychology and learn more about yourself and your mind.

Enjoy creative and artistic things as a hobby.

Overcome your tendency to "love 'em and leave 'em," for true happiness and peace of mind come only when you have learned emotional stability and to share in the joys of your romantic partner.

HOW CANCER PEOPLE CAN FIND PEACE, JOY, AND FULFILLMENT

You are apt to be too sensitive and easily hurt. This trait alone can cause you much grief and unhappiness in life. Try to insulate yourself by rationalizing people's actions and knowing that nothing can touch the real, inner you.

Try to overcome your shyness and reserve by deliberately forcing yourself to go out more socially. Take a course in dancing, singing, or public speaking, so you can learn how to function gracefully in any social environment.

You love your home and family and may let them become an escape from other activities. Give time and attention to your own social relationships and romantic affairs, and take some chances instead of always sidestepping new people and exciting new experiences.

Live less in the past and the future, and begin to live today. Share in the panorama of today's exciting world and feel a part of it, rather than sitting on the sidelines experiencing it vicariously through television.

Practice mind control to get control of your nerves, your moods, and fits of depression, and fill your life with studies, activities, and hobbies that make you forget your problems.

HOW LEO PEOPLE CAN FIND PEACE, JOY, AND FULFILLMENT

On the surface you seem to be living a joyous and radiantly ecstatic life. Your smiling face, your cheery and optimistic nature make people feel you are emotionally secure and don't have a problem on your mind. But this is not always true.

You are often lonely and unhappy. This can be due to the fact that your stars incline you to great ambitions and beautiful daydreams. When these do not come to pass you are apt to feel left out of things and it often brings you frustration and sorrow.

Learn to counteract this by not aiming at the stars; make your goals more realistic and attainable. Instead of trying to live up to the grandiose ideas of this royal sign of the zodiac, come down to earth and mix with the more ordinary mortals, and you will find that they have a good time, too. "Uneasy lies the head that wears a crown," someone has rightly said. Be one of those human beings who love to live for people and who enjoy sharing their love and joy with others; don't expect so much from your friends and don't isolate yourself by being self-centered and egotistical, as so many Leos are.

Cultivate faithfulness in love and try to be happy with a mate who gives you love and joy.

Keep your deep emotions under control and don't feel slighted or left out of things socially. You can't be everywhere at the same time, and you must not try to crowd your life.

To have more peace of mind and real happiness, control your ambitions, curb your temper and your tongue, meditate on higher mental and spiritual matters and less on the fleshpots of life.

HOW VIRGO PEOPLE CAN FIND PEACE, JOY, AND FULFILLMENT

Your retiring, modest nature often causes you to lose out on many of life's joys and pleasures. You are inclined to take the veil and isolate yourself from the common stream of life where much of the action and excitement exists. Share in this more and try to be more outgoing and extroverted. Many of your periods of loneliness and isolation could be due to your tendency to avoid meeting people and taking them on as friends.

Your ruling planet Mercury gives you a restless and highly nervous nature. This also increases your sensitivity and you may worry a great deal about things that will never happen. Live one day at a time and enjoy this day without projecting your worries and problems to the unknown future.

Try to be less critical and demanding of others. You are a perfectionist and apt to demand standards from your friends they can never live up to. Accept them as they are and try not to show your irritation at their inadequacies.

Cultivate your intellect and enjoy music, poetry, art, and good books; these will tide you over your periods of aloneness.

Fall in love and marry a suitable mate for much of your happiness and peace of mind come from emotional security.

Keep up your career aspirations if you are a Virgo woman for you have capabilities of carrying on a career and a home at the same time.

HOW LIBRA PEOPLE CAN FIND PEACE, JOY, AND FULFILLMENT

I could sum up the ideal situation for all Libra people by simply saying, "Fall in love and stay in love all the days of your life." This is because love is so vitally important in your life. Your ruling planet Venus gives you a romantic nature, and you are on an idealistic quest for the ideal soul mate.

It is these romantic yearnings, however, which often cause you emotional distress and make you so miserable. You are apt to tire of one lover and want another, and you must curb this tendency if you want to avoid heartache and misery.

Stop reacting so emotionally to everything that occurs in your life. Your unusual sensitivity causes you to be upset when things go wrong and this can unbalance you for hours and even days. Your sign is symbolized by the scales of balance; try to achieve this balance more frequently and you will have much more peace and happiness in your life.

You work best with other people as your sign rules marriage and partnerships. Align yourself with people who are socially agreeable and compatible. Try to marry someone who is born in a sign that is suitable to you. (See chapter three.)

Many of your emotional disturbances are triggered by your tendency to sarcasm and criticism of your friends and loved ones. You do not mean anything by this but people often misunderstand, and cannot imagine how anyone as sweet and charming as you are can suddenly be so venomous and sarcastic.

HOW SCORPIO PEOPLE CAN FIND PEACE, JOY, AND FULFILLMENT

Always remember your controlling planet is Mars which rules war. Mars gives you temperament, and this can degenerate into temper, impatience, and irritability which make you very hard to get along with. That is when the stinging scorpion side of your nature dominates.

You can emphasize the higher Scorpio nature, symbolized by the soaring eagle, and when you do this you are at your idealistic, witty, charming, and considerate best. Try to let this side of your nature rule you and you will never lack for friends and love.

As you are apt to be a catalytic force and change any environment you enter into, you have the power to upset the even tenor of a person's life and bring discord and friction into his environment. Strive to restrain your impulse to intrigue, gossip, and pry into the private affairs of others and you will have more joy and peace.

Get involved in a business where you can use your highly imaginative and creative nature, and your work will always be a source of delight to you. If you are in the wrong business, you are generally miserable and frustrated.

Use your terrific sex magnetism wisely and you will suffer less than if you give in to your highly emotional nature and become promiscuous and lascivious. Love and sexual expression should go together.

The two key words for you to remember when you are tempted to be irritated or blow your top are control and tolerance.

Yours is a fixed sign and you are apt to get into a rut in your work, your social life, and your pleasures; make it a point to change these habit patterns every once in a while and try to vary the monotony of your life by taking short trips, going away for the weekend, meeting new friends, or joining a new club where you can have a varied social life.

HOW SAGITTARIUS PEOPLE CAN FIND PEACE, JOY, AND FULFILLMENT

As your sign is a fire sign which gives you plenty of energy and vitality, you are inclined to constant activity. Never put yourself in any situation where you are stifled or frustrated. The keyword to your character is freedom. Even in marriage you must have a mate who understands this powerful drive and who is not too possessive and dominating.

Get involved in community activities where you can be recognized for your organizing ability—fund raising for charity, working for your church in a membership drive, or being involved in local politics. These can keep you in high gear all the time and give you an outlet for your vital creative energies.

Study some kind of philosophy and psychology so you will be able to organize your thinking and keep from being moody and depressed.

Have close friends you can share a limited social life with, go to parties, and attend dances and social events that keep you happy and occupied.

Your Jupiter planet gives you good fortune as a rule if you can keep yourself on the high level of creativity you desire. Cultivate hobbies in art, music, decorating, or designing, and you will be able to stand up under your strenuous job demands.

Try to travel frequently for this sign rules travel, and have a plan that encompasses visiting foreign countries over the years. You usually have unusual experiences and meet interesting people through this form of activity that could bring you pleasure and profit.

HOW CAPRICORN PEOPLE CAN FIND PEACE, JOY, AND FULFILLMENT

Your sign is often called the "loner" because you are inclined to shut other people out of the intimate circle of your personal life. This tendency often causes you to feel lonely and rejected. You can correct this by mingling more with other people socially and expanding your range of acquaintances.

A frequent cause of discontent and unhappiness with those born in Capricorn is the tendency to aim too high, and sometimes set goals that are difficult, if not impossible to achieve. This makes you feel frustrated and inadequate. To overcome this aim at smaller goals first, and then raise your sights ever higher when you have achieved these small goals.

Try to cultivate more patience with people and realize that everyone has weaknesses. Don't give in so frequently to temper and irritability for this only adds to your general unhappiness.

Saturn, your ruling planet, is known as a harsh disciplinarian. Your life may be hard and laborious, and you may at times feel that fate is pitted against you and is trying to destroy you. Realize that Saturn rewards those who are able to achieve mastery and control of their minds and tempers and gives them fulfillment and satisfaction, as a rule, in the years past forty and fifty. So don't give up hope when things go wrong.

Try not to make money and material goals your only measuring stick of success. You need balance in your life and should cultivate interests in creative fields and religion.

HOW AQUARIUS PEOPLE CAN FIND
PEACE, JOY, AND FULFILLMENT

Your main source of annoyance may well come from being so misunderstood by most people. Your sign, ruled by Uranus, often makes you different from the ordinary person. You cannot conform to what most people call "normal" actions, and you are inclined to make your own social and moral laws. This makes you rebellious of restrictions and you have a desire to go your own way and ignore the clamor of the multitudes.

You may well be a genius, for so many Aquarians do achieve fame and fortune, but this may also cause you to be lonely and unhappy. There are few people who can stand the frenzied pace you set and they may drop out of your life rather than make the effort to keep up with you.

If you want to avoid many unhappy moments, try to cultivate more consideration for the feelings of others. Be on time when you make an appointment; consider the feelings of others in love and marriage, rather than think only about yourself.

Overcome your tendency to vacillation and change. This sign often marries two or three times, unable to make a decision as to what they want.

It is good to be idealistic, but you are living in a world of imperfections and limitations, so adjust your mind to the constant changes, disappointments, and frustrations which are a part of every person's life. You will then be happier and more at peace with yourself and your fellow men.

HOW PISCES PEOPLE CAN FIND
PEACE, JOY, AND FULFILLMENT

Your highly sensitive and sympathetic nature makes you suffer for unfortunates around you. You are always trying to help others and sometimes you neglect your own welfare. Change some of this sympathy into concern for your family and yourself, and then indulge your charitable spirit and do for others.

Try to handle money and material success with a little more care than is usual with Pisceans. You have the ability to make money but your overly generous nature frequently makes you spend it on others. Prepare for future security as your nature hates being dependent on others for support, especially in old age.

Give plenty of time and attention to romantic and marital affairs. Pisces happiness is usually built around some other person you love. Be sure to select a compatible mate. (See chapter three for compatible signs for love and marriage.)

Surround yourself with beautiful things in your home. A home will mean a great deal to you in the future for peace of mind and happiness. Try to establish a comfortable setting so you can relax and entertain a few select friends. Your sociable nature will attract many good friends during your life.

Try not to make the typical Pisces mistakes; this is called the house of self-undoing because most of your misfortunes can be laid at your own doorstep. You should avoid overindulgence in smoking, drinking, gambling, or other negative habits.

11

How Your Stars Can Help You Develop Artistic and Creative Talents

Thousands of people have hidden creative and artistic potentials which they never develop. Often they are so busy preparing for a profession that they neglect their inner promptings to create something artistic and beautiful that will give them personal satisfaction and possibly bring them fame and fortune.

An interesting example was that of an artist known simply as Grandma Moses who was born in the sign of Virgo. Frail and sickly and given up to die by doctors, Grandma Moses began dabbling with paints to while away the tedium of the day. Soon she was creating little primitives which she gave away as presents to friends. Before very long her paintings of quaint New England landscapes were selling for as much as $5,000 each. A First Lady bought one for the White House.

But the most important side effect of this sudden discovery of latent artistic and creative talent was the fact that this frail, sickly old lady suddenly blossomed with new vigor and vitality and outlasted most of her relatives, living to be one hundred and one years of age.

What are your hidden artistic and creative potentials, according to your sign? Each sign has been given some special talent and you can bring out this hidden genius by studying your stars and seeing how you can develop this creative genius.

These creative talents are not limited to the field of painting; they include invention, composing, designing clothes, interior decorating, cosmetology, writing stories, articles, poetry, and drama for the theater or television, sculpting, architecture, landscape gardening, acting, singing, dancing, directing and producing for the theater, and a host of other creative talents which bring outstanding success to thousands of people.

HOW ARIES PEOPLE CAN DEVELOP THEIR CREATIVE TALENTS

This first sign of the zodiac, ruling the brain and intellect, should be the leader in all fields, not only in business but in the creative and artistic professions.

To bring out your latent talents in the artistic field, follow your natural intuition. You will know, with a little careful analysis of your preferences, whether you have a gift for writing novels, plays, or factual articles. You will feel drawn to music or painting, but these artistic endeavors all require study and hard work. Aries generally follow the path of least resistance, so take into consideration that you must study and prepare yourself for any of these artistic vocations.

You also possess a great deal of drama in your makeup, and you could very easily express your creative genius in the fields of acting, directing, stage managing, costume designing, or any other work connected with the theater, television, or motion pictures.

Writing for the stage and motion pictures is also a natural talent for Aries-born. Thornton Wilder, renowned dramatist, was born in this sign. Clare Boothe Luce, whose famous play *The Women* which was later made into a motion picture, was also an Arian. One of our great modern dramatists, Tennessee Williams, was also born in this most gifted of all signs, as was Lowell Thomas, producer, traveler, and commentator.

Aries men are often inventive in a mechanical sense. You may have a hidden genius to invent some object that can make you a million dollars.

Aries women are gifted also in interior decorating and have a good sense of color and design.

As an actor, you excel in projecting magnetism and drama in your personality. Some of the early motion-picture leaders were Arians, including Charlie Chaplin, Harold Lloyd, Mary Pickford, and Gloria Swanson, as well as later stars Joan Crawford, Bette Davis, William Holden, Spencer Tracy, and many others.

HOW TAURUS PEOPLE CAN DEVELOP
THEIR CREATIVE TALENTS

Taurus people have a great deal of hidden talent in an artistic way. They are generally interested in art, music, poetry, and literature. Although the sign itself rules the second house (over money, lands, houses, and investments), most Taureans have a natural instinct for the creative and beautiful.

With Venus your ruling planet (and this has to do with women, beauty, love, and art), you are naturally attracted to creative things dealing with fashion designing, jewelry and objects of female adornment, cosmetology and cosmetics in all different branches, interior decorating, and landscape gardening.

Perhaps one of the most obvious talents for Taureans is that of music and singing. This sign rules the voice and throat, and many singers were born in this sign, including Dean Martin, Bing Crosby, Kate Smith, Pat Boone, Shirley Temple, and Carol Burnett. This sign is a big money-maker and can succeed in the field of music, art, and literature.

Writing is a natural for Taureans also. Shakespeare, who was born on April 25, exemplifies the type of imagination these lucky people possess. In the field of inspirational writing they also excel; Archbishop Fulton J. Sheen was born in Taurus.

Other writers born in Taurus were Dr. Benjamin Spock, Philip Wylie, Katherine Anne Porter, and President Harry Truman who wrote of his White House years in very excellent, pungent prose.

HOW GEMINI PEOPLE CAN DEVELOP
THEIR CREATIVE TALENTS

This most gifted of all the twelve signs in the zodiac can apply itself to any and all artistic endeavors with a great degree of success. In fact, one of the big difficulties for those born in this multitalented sign is to make a choice between their many talents.

If you are a Gemini, your biggest problem is to choose one or two artistic fields you want to follow. Being dual in nature, you will probably try your hand at art and music at the same time. There is nothing wrong in this if you make up your mind you want both gifts. Or you may choose writing and composing as your vocation in the artistic field. You can easily achieve success in the music field for your facile mind can easily write lyrics as well as compose magnificent music. Some great composers and musicians were born in Gemini.

The men born in Gemini often go into architecture and with their artistic minds and mathematical sense become great successes in that field.

Gemini women often choose the literary field, sometimes as excellent writers for women's magazines and very often as editors for women's publications or in the book publishing field. Their excellent sense of criticism makes them good as literary or music critics.

In the field of satirical wit and humor Geminis have no peers. (Dorothy Parker was born in Gemini.) They have expressive minds, a good sense of communication through the written or spoken word, and are excellent as TV newscasters or commentators.

The noted partygiver, Elsa Maxwell, who associated with the highest ranks of society on both continents as well as with royalty, wrote highly amusing articles and columns on social activities.

The Duchess of Windsor, another talented Gemini, wrote her dramatic story, *The Heart Has Its Reasons*, in collaboration with the Duke of Windsor who was a Cancerian.

Terence Rattigan, the playwright, was born in this sign, as was Herman Wouk, the famous novelist.

Both men and women born in Gemini often excel as interior decorators, dress designers, and makeup specialists in films or for the theater.

In the fields of poetry and philosophical writing, Geminis show their true genius. The transcendental philosopher Ralph Waldo Emerson was born in Gemini, as were Dr. Norman Vincent Peale and poet Walt Whitman.

HOW CANCER PEOPLE CAN DEVELOP THEIR CREATIVE TALENTS

Cancer is ruled by the moon which gives Cancerians great powers of creativity and imagination. They make excellent artists, writers, musicians, and inventors. They often excel as actors.

To develop your creative talents find out what you are most attracted to in the way of mental and intellectual gifts.

You often choose an artistic vocation but are dissuaded from following it because of the influence of your parents or some friend. You must listen to your own intuition which will accurately tell you which creative field you can succeed in.

Music, singing, composing, conducting, and arranging are all excellent for the Cancer-born to follow. Your extreme sensitivity, your acute sense of hearing, and your emotional responses all fit you for this highly specialized artistic field. This, of course, often takes several years of intensive training and studying, and that is where you may fail to follow through. You are apt to lose interest and change your mind after beginning your studies, and your impatience makes it difficult to finish your studies. (Gian-Carlo Menotti, a modern operatic composer, was born in Cancer.)

You are apt to be too impatient for painting or sculpting as you like to see immediate results and this isn't possible in these fields.

Acting is ideally suited to your temperament and emotional volatility. Some of our great stars were born in this sign, including James Cagney, Barbara Stanwyck, and Olivia de Havilland.

Perhaps you can try your talents at writing romantic novels for you have a sense of drama and romance that gives you a special flair as an author. Margaret Mitchell, who wrote *Gone With the Wind*, and Pearl S. Buck, who wrote *The Good Earth* and many other stories with an oriental background, were Cancerians.

HOW LEO PEOPLE CAN DEVELOP THEIR CREATIVE TALENTS

Leo people excel in any field they select for their artistic endeavors. As this sign is so outgoing and dramatic, they are very good in the theater and motion pictures, as actors, directors, and producers. They are leaders and managers in whatever field they decide to exercise their creative talents. They usually get to the top because of their aggressive tendencies and their desire to succeed.

Leo people often go into the general fields of entertainment and amusement and become highly successful. In the performing arts, they make good musicians, singers, dancers, and actors. In the fields of instruction, they make excellent teachers of music, art, sculpting, acting, and dancing. Sometimes they become choreographers for big Broadway shows or motion pictures where they can use their executive ability and their qualities of leadership and authority.

Often Leo people find their place in the field of lecturing or working with travelogues which they show in theaters with descriptive comments.

As novelists and short story writers, Leo people usually deal in strong, dramatic themes, and sometimes they write historical novels about royalty and the upper social classes. As they are very conscious of social caste, they sometimes go into writing columns on society, manners and etiquette, and things connected with members of royalty. Jacqueline Kennedy Onassis is typical of the Leo who strives to rise to the highest levels of society, and it might be said that her great creative gift lies in being a charming hostess in an international setting.

HOW VIRGO PEOPLE CAN DEVELOP THEIR CREATIVE TALENTS

Virgo is a highly talented sign as it is ruled by the planet of the higher mind, Mercury. If you were born in Virgo you can easily discover your latent artistic and creative talents and achieve outstanding success.

Perhaps the greatest talent possessed by Virgo is in the field of writing. Some of the most outstanding authors were born in this gifted sign, including O. Henry, Bret Harte, Upton Sinclair, Leo Tolstoi, H. G. Wells, Theodore Dreiser, F. Scott Fitzgerald, H. L. Mencken, and Robert Benchley.

As musicians and composers many Virgos become proficient and capable. Their minds, however, are more literal and practical than fanciful and inventive, and they often become good technical musicians but seldom become geniuses in that field.

As artists, sculptors, and designers, you can achieve outstanding success, as you have a good eye for form, color, and design. In women's fashions you would excel as you have advanced ideas and a sense of what is artistic and beautiful.

Virgos are often too modest and shy to become great actors, but there have been some exceptions: Greta Garbo was born in this sign as were Joan Blondell, Claudette Colbert, and Fred Mac-

Murray; but Virgos prefer to be behind the artistic scenes, as writers, directors, and managers of actors and singers.

As cosmetologists and cosmetic experts, Virgos excel. One of the famous Westmore brothers was born in this sign. Virgos often win prizes for hairstyling and are excellent working in beauty salons or in connection with figure building, diet and health, and preparing artistic and healthful menus. Gayelord Hauser, author on health foods and lecturer, was born in Virgo.

HOW LIBRA PEOPLE CAN DEVELOP THEIR CREATIVE TALENTS

As Venus is your ruling planet it inclines you to being artistic and creative quite naturally. You love everything beautiful and harmonious and are at your happiest when you can be in surroundings that reflect beauty.

This sign makes you fond of poetry, music, and art. You have special talents for poetry and writing and could easily become an outstanding author in the field of romance and drama. Faith Baldwin, the noted novelist was born in Libra. Truman Capote, famous author of *In Cold Blood* and *Breakfast at Tiffany's*, was also a Libran. Arthur Miller, famous dramatist, was born in this sign also.

As an interior decorator, landscape gardener, or fashion designer in women's clothes, you would excel with your eye for color and your sense of proportion and balance.

Venus people are also excellent in the field of jewelry designing, hairstyling, and general cosmetics. Anything that has to do with beautifying women or making the home more beautiful and artistic belongs in the category of the Libra talents.

The acting profession is often chosen by Libra women for they are usually beautiful in face and form and have a special talent for arousing emotions in a spectator in the theater, TV, and motion pictures. In past times, Eleanora Duse and Sarah Bernhardt were Librans, and in more recent times, actresses Greer Garson, Constance Bennett, Janet Gaynor, Carole Lombard, Miriam Hopkins, and Helen Hayes were born in this gifted sign.

HOW SCORPIO PEOPLE CAN DEVELOP THEIR CREATIVE TALENTS

Scorpio's creative genius usually expresses itself in the realm of ideas, in chemical discoveries, scientific research, and inventions. Scorpios are excellent in the fields of advertising and commercial art. They are excellent directors for television drama or stage productions. They are usually the brains behind big musical festivals and operatic presentations as their minds work well in grasping overall concepts of presenting a dramatic work to the public. They are geniuses in planning campaigns for raising money through charitable organizations, and in the entertainment world. Billy Graham was born in Scorpio and well exemplifies the Scorpio talent for massive public presentations of religious spectacles on a theatrical scale that outdo any stage production.

Scorpios are also excellent at inventing new gadgets for everyday use that could well make them a million dollars.

They also make good architects, chemical engineers, and landscape gardeners. Jonas Salk was born in Scorpio and his creative genius produced the polio vaccine that bears his name.

Mme. Marie Curie was also born in Scorpio and her creative genius, with that of her husband, helped discover radium.

Ignace Paderewski, noted composer, pianist, and statesman, was born in Scorpio, as was Marianne Moore, famous poetess. Actresses Vivien Leigh and Hedy Lamarr were Scorpio-born.

HOW SAGITTARIUS PEOPLE CAN DEVELOP THEIR CREATIVE TALENTS

The creative genius of Sagittarius is best expressed through the medium of the spoken or written word and also through musical compositions. They are good at communicating their creative ideas to the public and often become writers, composers, humorists, poets, philosophers, explorers, and columnists.

As statesmen they often use the higher creative minds that most Sagittarians possess. Two famous instances of this great power were Sir Winston Churchill and Benjamin Disraeli. Not only was Churchill a great statesman, leader, and speaker but he also had great talent as an artist and writer.

As a rule Sagittarians are good at expressing themselves through the written word. You could become a famous author or poet. Some famous authors born in this sign were John Milton, Gustave Flaubert, Mark Twain, and in more recent times, Erskine Caldwell, Noel Coward, Willa Cather, and Arthur Brisbane.

Poet John Greenleaf Whittier was born in Sagittarius, and Beethoven was also born in this gifted sign.

The famous humorist, artist, and author James Thurber was also born in Sagittarius.

You can see that there is a wide range of Sagittarius creativity by seeing those born in your sign. You can also excel in invention, painting, and interior decorating.

HOW CAPRICORN PEOPLE CAN DEVELOP THEIR CREATIVE TALENTS

As Capricorn people are the most ambitious in the entire zodiac, it is natural that many of them find their way into the most artistic and creative fields of endeavor.

They have the patience and perseverance to succeed in commercial arts, but they also make very fine draftsmen, portrait painters, and architects.

However, it is in the field of music and acting that many Capricorns find their truest creative expression. The rock and roll singer Elvis Presley was born in the sign of Capricorn.

As writers of fiction, Capricorn people show a great deal of imagination and are highly realistic and dramatic in their use of words. Edgar Allan Poe was typical of this Capricorn talent. Novelist James Baldwin is also a Capricorn. Rudyard Kipling, Louis Bromfield, and Jack London were born in this fortunate sign.

When it comes to such things as interior decorating, cosmetology, fashion designing, and sculpting, Capricorns can succeed, but they usually prefer testing their creative talents in the more prosaic and practical fields of advertising and commercial art. They are also excellent as editors and advertising directors in newspapers and magazines.

HOW AQUARIUS PEOPLE CAN DEVELOP
THEIR CREATIVE TALENTS

Creativity of a very high order is a natural attribute of those born in this most gifted of all signs. More geniuses were born in this talented sign and it is said that most of the people in the Hall of Fame are Aquarians.

Your greatest talents lie in the realm of inspirational ideas. This can apply to inventions, electronics, aviation, computers, radio and television, and the automotive field. It also includes designing, inventing, and promoting all such products. These are said to be the Aquarian age inventions, and as this age unfolds more and more Aquarians will come to the forefront in space age exploration and inventions.

It is interesting to note that Charles Lindbergh, a typical Aquarian, made the first solo flight across the Atlantic in 1927.

It is also interesting to see that Thomas Edison, one of our greatest inventors, was born in the sign of Aquarius. His motion picture and electric light, out of his three hundred inventions, set the stage for the fantastic twentieth century we have inherited.

If you were born in Aquarius you have a natural gift for all forms of art, music, designing, interior decorating, chemical and mechanical inventions, as well as having talent for the highest literary creations in the publishing field.

Norman Rockwell, the artist, was an Aquarian.

The following authors from the past were Aquarians: Charles Dickens, Lewis Carroll, Robert Burns, and Lord Byron. In our own day, Norman Mailer, James Michener, James Joyce, S. J. Perelman, and Gertrude Stein were born in Aquarius.

You can develop any art form successfully for you have a highly imaginative mind and think in terms of the original, unusual, and advanced forms of creative art.

HOW PISCES PEOPLE CAN DEVELOP
THEIR CREATIVE TALENTS

Pisceans have inherited artistic and creative talents that are almost as great as their Aquarius brothers.

If you were born in this sign you have a natural flair for beauty and adornment. The women make excellent designers of gowns and hats. They are also good interior decorators and landscape gardeners. They have great potentials for poetry, music, and acting.

The Pisces men incline toward creativity in the fields of chemistry, physics, and the healing arts. They often design machinery for hospitals and institutions. They make good as architects and designers of X-ray, dental, and obstetric machinery.

In the literary field Pisceans have no peers as they are highly imaginative and produce literature that is often highly idealistic and deep. James Russell Lowell, Victor Hugo, Henry Wadsworth Longfellow, Henrik Ibsen, and Elizabeth Barrett Browning were some of our talented Pisceans from the past. In our modern age, William L. Shirer and Mickey Spillane were born in Pisces.

12

Your Ultimate Destiny According to Your Birthsign

In ancient India and Tibet, where astrology dominated and still does influence the lives of millions of people, it was believed that the zodiac was a great wheel of fortune and that people were born in the various signs of the zodiac to fill a definite karmic pattern of ultimate destiny. (Karma simply means action and reaction; when your actions are good, the reactions will be good.)

Each sign has been given handicaps that will make a person stronger if he learns how to meet life's challenges and overcome the misfortunes and obstacles he meets on life's path to spiritual fulfillment.

Also, each sign has been given strengths and virtues that will aid him in achieving his life goal if he uses them. Each person is a free agent and may choose either the upward path to a great destiny or the lower path to failure and disaster. No one sign is better or worse than the others.

Many people point out the fact that two men will be born on the exact same day, time, and place, and one might become a president, while the other becomes a miserable failure. This, they claim, disproves astrology. They often point out examples like Hitler, and say that people born on April 20, the same day as Hitler, do not become criminals, and many of them in fact are geniuses who help humanity.

There is a simple explanation in karmic astrology of this seeming discrepancy. Each person born on this wheel of fate, which is the zodiac with the twelve signs, is given an opportunity either to develop his star-given destiny or to shirk his responsibilities and choose the downward path to disaster and failure. Hitler chose his own path of destiny, and his evil genius was responsible for the deaths of millions of people. If he had chosen the upward path, his star-given destiny could have been one of fulfillment for the German people and peace for the world.

Which path of destiny will you choose? Following are the different karmic destinies for the twelve signs of the zodiac. Study these and learn of your built-in weaknesses, and also the strengths that can counteract them. Then strive to achieve the highest goals and live by the most idealistic concepts you can conceive of and you will be certain to attract your ultimate destiny according to the stars.

YOUR ULTIMATE DESTINY IF BORN IN ARIES

Your potentials for greatness are enormous, but so are your karmic weaknesses. You know your good points, so let's dwell a little on those negative things in your sign that might keep you from achieving an ultimate destiny of health, happiness, and prosperity.

Mars, your ruling planet, makes you very ambitious, but it also gives you a tendency to a quick temper and to hasty and impulsive actions. You act without thinking of the consequences of your actions and this might lead you to take steps that could lead to disaster.

Being a natural-born leader can also be a negative point, if you push this too far and want to dominate and bulldoze everyone around you.

You are apt to be selfish and disregard the rights and opinions of others, and this tendency can lead to clashes between you and your family and close friends. Learn to curb this self-centeredness and realize that you must respect the rights and opinions of others some of the time.

Karmically you were born in the sign of Aries to give you a chance to discipline yourself and overcome some of your faults. Mars makes you combative and dominating. In love and marriage especially, you must guard against being a tyrant and thinking you have to have your own way all the time.

Another fault with your Aries character is that you are aflame with inspiration when something new comes along and occupies your attention. But then you just as quickly cool on this new interest and often abandon it, never really accomplishing the great things that should be your ultimate destiny.

Adjectives like willful, rash, impetuous, pugnacious, selfish, stubborn, and cruel are apt to fit you when you do not strive to rise to the highest levels of aspiration for those born in this wonderful sign.

YOUR ULTIMATE DESTINY IF BORN IN TAURUS

You have the power to achieve ultimate greatness through the wonderful qualities nature has bestowed on you if you were born in the sign of Taurus. But you also have those built-in weaknesses that can make your life one of frustration, failure, and misery.

Venus, your controlling planet, rules love and peace. You are naturally a lovable and peaceful person, but like the bull which is the symbol of your sign, you can easily become enraged, ferocious, and destructive.

Your love can often degenerate into licentiousness and animalism. When someone opposes you or has opinions opposite your own, your sweet, gentle nature can deteriorate into stubbornness, hostility, and anger. Your rages are terrifying and you can be as destructive as the proverbial "bull in the china shop."

Your nature is fixed and unyielding, which is fine when you have a positive and constructive idea, but when it comes to a negative condition in your life, you should try to change this tendency to remain adamant and fixed for it can lead to staying in work that is wrong or living in a home that is not comfortable. You should develop the habit of making changes more easily and adapting to changes with greater readiness.

You are inclined to love the home and children, but your nature often makes you a strict parent and a stern disciplinarian. Try to cultivate more patience and understanding for the weaknesses of those who are in your family or who work with you. You like good food and high living, but this can degenerate into gluttony, overeating and overdrinking, to the great detriment of your health and life.

YOUR ULTIMATE DESTINY
IF BORN IN GEMINI

Perhaps the most charming side of your character is the duality that makes you a sparkling and interesting personality. But it can also be your most deadly defect; it leads to vacillation, indecision, and inability to follow one course of action that might bring success and fulfillment.

Your wonderful wit makes you a charming social companion, until that wit deteriorates and becomes sarcasm and cutting satire. If it is directed against another, it can make that individual your most bitter enemy.

In love and marriage this strange duality may cause you many heartaches. You rush into love affairs without knowing if you are really in love, then you change your mind the next day and have to get out of it. This often causes you to be thought of as being ruthless, cold, and unemotional.

You are ruled by Mercury, the mental planet, but sometimes you are too mental and tend to ignore the other departments of your life. Too much concentration of the mental type often causes you to overwork and bring yourself to the verge of a nervous collapse.

You are good at handling people and often get into positions of power and authority, but this can also work against you; you can be too demanding and exacting of others and you may be regarded as tyrannical and hardhearted.

You often become extremely moody and depressed; at times you may even think of suicide. You must build more mental and emotional stability to counteract this tendency to morbidity and melancholia. A broken love affair often takes you to the verge of mental and physical collapse. Work to strengthen your mind by merging the two opposing sides of your twin nature.

YOUR ULTIMATE DESTINY
IF BORN IN CANCER

Your ruling planet, the moon, makes you highly sensitive and reflective. It increases your powers of imagination and often causes you to see phantoms of fear for the future that have no real basis in fact. You must strive to become more emotionally secure and turn this oversensitivity into confidence and self-reliance.

Your inclination to be reserved and cautious can often degenerate into inaction and indecision that could cause you to miss out on many opportunities for progress in your life. You have a tendency to put things off until tomorrow; you fear investing in property for fear you cannot meet the payments; you anticipate sickness, accident, insanity, divorce, and disaster in your relations with your family and friends. This negative side of your nature often robs you of much of the joy of living.

Your karma seems to be in connection with those close to you in your own family. You love the home and children, and yet it is in these areas of action and reaction that many of your most vexatious problems arise. Your maternal or paternal concern for your children may turn into domination and tyranny. You may drive your own children away by being too critical, too demanding, too moralistic, and high-principled. Try to tone down the nagging and criticism of your mate and your children, and your devotion and concern will then be more emphatic.

You can have many friends and a joyous life destiny if you develop your higher intuition and follow it to your high goals in life.

YOUR ULTIMATE DESTINY IF BORN IN LEO

Your sign is often called a lucky sign, but there are many built-in weaknesses and tendencies that can rob you of much peace and happiness. As the sun is your ruling planet it makes you very ambitious and desirous of rising to very high levels of achievement.

Sometimes this ambition can deteriorate into grandiose schemes that are impossible to fulfill and the disappointment and frustration that frequently ensue can make you miserable.

Your desire to go to the top may make you ruthless, selfish, and unconcerned about the rights and interests of others. Try to curb your impetuosity, your temper, and your impatience with people, and cultivate more of a sense of inner harmony and tranquillity.

Your sign is called the royal sign in the zodiac, but remember that there is a saying about royalty, "uneasy lies the head that wears a crown." You may achieve high goals, but do not do so by sacrificing peace of mind, honor, integrity, and spiritual values. Temper your ambitions with the desire to share your good with the world and to help those who are less fortunate than yourself.

You have tremendous charm and magnetism which draw many people to you as friends, but you are also apt to toss your friends aside if they no longer suit your soaring ambitions. This often leads to instability and insincerity. Most Leos are generous and magnanimous, but the karmic pattern is sometimes selfishness and miserliness, hating to spend money on others, and trying to take advantage of them in business and social activities.

YOUR ULTIMATE DESTINY IF BORN IN VIRGO

Your practical and highly intelligent nature often makes you miss out on some of the simple pleasures of life. You are always striving to achieve perfection and ultimate greatness. Try to be more tolerant of the weaknesses of others. Also avoid criticizing them and finding fault with the weaknesses of your mate, your children, and your friends.

The karma for Virgo-born seems to be tied in with their ruling planet Mercury, which governs the mind and the nervous system. They often worry and overwork and have nervous breakdowns. They must strive to achieve mental and emotional stability.

You are inclined to be rather cold, unemotional, and unresponsive in love and marriage. Strive to show more warmth and affection. Your reserve and dignity should be put aside occasionally for fun and relaxation. Your tendency to want to be alone much of the time may cause you to become an isolated personality with eccentric habits that estrange you from people.

Your concern for food, health, and diet is apt to be overstressed, making you a faddist and causing psychosomatic ills that are based on your emotional upsets. Try to build normal dietary habits and avoid overemphasis on things connected with your health and diet. Get plenty of rest and relaxation, as Mercury frequently makes you nervous, tense, and irritated at the little vexatious problems in life.

Avoid being the perpetual schoolteacher, pointing out the mistakes in grammar your friends or relatives make. This tendency often makes people think of you as being critical and dominating.

Cultivate more mental poise and inner serenity and you will fulfill your karmic destiny more easily.

YOUR ULTIMATE DESTINY
IF BORN IN LIBRA

Your karmic pattern is one of peace and love fulfillment. However, this innate desire in your Libra nature often becomes sadly disrupted by the built-in weaknesses for those born in this beautiful sign of the zodiac. Venus, your ruling planet, makes you sensitive to anything that is ugly, harsh, coarse, and vulgar. Your reaction to discord and friction in your environment is apt to be extremely severe and may upset the delicate balance which is the keynote of your character.

Strive to be less sensitive and react less to the external situations which distress you and which you cannot change.

Your strong point is your romantic and loving nature, and yet this often is the very thing that creates all your problems. You are apt to be in love with love rather than with a person, and this may lead you to a perpetual quest for love fulfillment. You may develop fickleness, jealousy, suspicion, and possessiveness of your love partner.

As the symbol of the scales is your sign's trademark, you are very likely to let your emotions become unbalanced and this tendency leads to irritations and friction instead of peace. It often makes you sarcastic and cutting in your remarks and makes people turn against you. You want love and attention, but you are apt to let this degenerate into possessiveness and selfishness.

You have a desire to help the unfortunate and underprivileged, but this can lead to neglecting your own family and friends. Eleanor Roosevelt was a typical Libran who took care of everyone else's social problems but neglected her own family's needs.

YOUR ULTIMATE DESTINY
IF BORN IN SCORPIO

Your ruling planet Mars gives you a great deal of combativeness, aggression, and determination. This can sometimes bring you into open conflict with those who are close to you in the home and in business. You must be careful that your excessive energy and fire do not degenerate into qualities of dominance, cruelty, and insubordination.

Your love of intrigue and gossip often create problems among your friends. You are apt to enjoy seeing them squirm, and you must avoid entanglements in love and friendship that could bring you enmity and opposition.

Your determination to succeed and rise to the top of the ladder of success can often turn into ruthlessness and dishonesty. You sometimes don't care how many people you step on to get there, but this can have repercussions and lead to many problems in your future.

You demand loyalty from friends and loved ones, but when wrongly used this often can be tyranny and domination. You have a tendency to be jealous and possessive of those you love and to try to suppress them and limit their social actions. This can make people think of you as being brutal and cruel.

One of the weapons frequently used by Scorpios is lashing out with sarcasm and cutting criticism when they are opposed or denied something. This often results in secret enemies who may try to destroy them.

Control your temper and your tongue, overcome your tendency to want to have your own way all the time, and you will probably have a much happier life and avoid suffering and unhappiness.

YOUR ULTIMATE DESTINY IF BORN IN SAGITTARIUS

Even your lucky sign of Sagittarius has some karmic debits connected with its good fortune. Your idealism and desire for ultimate perfection are apt to be unfulfilled, and you become moody and depressed and tend to give up rather easily. You must strive for more persistence and lower your sights to achievable goals first, before striving for heights that you may not be able to scale at present.

Your desire for freedom and independence often leads to rebellion against society's mores and the conventional institutions that govern social conduct, business, and marriage. Strive to conform in this respect for the rebel often is left on the outer periphery of society's activities and you could become isolated, lonely, and unhappy.

Your tendency to trust people and be honest often causes you to be hurt by others. It might be good to develop a little more caution in dealing with strangers and not trust everyone you meet.

It is in love and marriage that you are apt to meet your worst karmic challenges. It is difficult to attract a mate who understands your desire to be free, even though married. This can lead to confusion and discord and break up your marriage.

You have a tendency to be moody, depressed, and melancholy very often. You must build more inner invariability and spirituality, so you are able to meet life's challenges with peace and equanimity. You usually achieve a high and honorable destiny if you fully live up to your star-given potentials.

YOUR ULTIMATE DESTINY IF BORN IN CAPRICORN

The karmic destiny for those born in this powerful sign is often very strong and sometimes unfortunate. Saturn, the planet that rules this sign, is said to severely try its subjects and then, if they are strong enough to keep from breaking down, they ultimately achieve the greatest of all destinies.

What happened to Richard M. Nixon is typical of the obstacles and problems that Saturn throws in the way of those born in Capricorn. President Woodrow Wilson, also born in Capricorn, experienced his own personal defeat in the League of Nations; he survived his personal crisis but suffered much public humiliation and shame from the calumnies heaped upon him by the public.

You will have to avoid many things that might tend to destroy you. Avoid being overly ambitious and strive to enjoy small personal achievements first before going to the summits your Capricorn nature craves. Give more time to family and friends, for you are apt to be cold, stern, aloof, and uncompromising in your relations to others.

Your love of power can degenerate into tyranny and a dictatorial attitude toward your family and friends. (Stalin was born in Capricorn.)

Your desire for money, fame, and power often leads to deceptions, misrepresentation, and ruthlessness in business. Some of the world's richest men were born in Capricorn, but their karma is usually burdensome. Aristotle Onassis, a typical Capricorn, was too busy making billions to pay much attention to his son. When he died tragically in an airplane crash, the elder Onassis said, "I would give my entire fortune to have my son back."

Howard Hughes, another billionaire Capricorn, attained everything in the world he ever wanted at the expense of his mental and physical health and peace of mind.

Elvis Presley made millions with his Capricorn shrewdness and talent, but suffered agony when he lost his beloved mother. His career had absorbed him completely and his karma caught up with him.

Mohammed Ali, another Capricorn, could never face failure and defeat and he won every one of his fights except the last one because he shut everything else out of his life but his burning ambition to be number one. At this writing he's on the comeback trail and is considerably more humble.

Don't sacrifice your peace of mind, integrity, honor, and soul's tranquillity for the wealth and prestige of this world, for your karma is to lose out on the most valuable things in life if you let your ambitions destroy you. "For what shall it profit a man if he gain the whole world and lose his own soul?"

YOUR ULTIMATE DESTINY IF BORN IN AQUARIUS

The greatness of Aquarians is often offset by the karma they have to pay for their star-given destinies. They are often tested beyond endurance by their life experiences. Sometimes their indifference and independence cause them to lose the ones they love most. Often they are so engrossed in their own sense of importance that they ignore their friends and relatives.

If you are an Aquarian realize that you can rise to a position of greatness, but ask yourself the question, "Do I want to pay the price for fame and fortune?" You will be asked to sacrifice your peace of mind; your personal happiness may suffer, your loved ones may desert you, and even your health may suffer. It is sometimes better to settle for a less spectacular destiny than to sacrifice yourself on the altar of greatness.

Aquarius is the most often-married sign of the entire zodiac, and this is one of the karmic crosses you must bear unless you learn how to control your emotions and become more loving, sympathetic, and understanding of your mate. Zsa Zsa Gabor, her sister Eva, Clark Gable, John Barrymore, and Lana Turner were born in this sign, and each was married several times. I have counseled hundreds of people born in Aquarius and find that the department of love is the most vulnerable in their lives and causes them much suffering and anguish until they learn how to master their karma.

Your restless nature makes it difficult for you to settle in one home, and you may have a tendency to travel and change all through your life. This can be upsetting emotionally and cause many problems.

Your ruling planet Uranus gives you a high-pitched, nervous temperament. You lose your temper quickly, are apt to be impatient, critical of another's shortcomings, quickly bored, and demand instant obedience and compliance with your every whim. You create most of your own problems until you learn that your karma is one of suffering and punishment for disobeying the great natural laws of the universe, laws of decency, honesty, integrity, and loving-kindness toward all other human beings. Only then do you become the true humanitarian and genius that your stars destined you to be.

YOUR ULTIMATE DESTINY
IF BORN IN PISCES

You were born in the sign of the zodiac called the karmic house of misfortune and self-undoing. Like the Aquarians, you have been given latent genius and sometimes you have to suffer and sacrifice your personal happiness, peace of mind, and health to bring it out.

One of your main faults which causes you much indecision and lack of positive action is the fact that you are dual in nature, very much like the sign of Gemini. Your sign is symbolized by the two fish, one swimming upstream, the other downstream. One side of your nature is lofty, idealistic, and strives to achieve a great destiny. The other side is earthbound, selfish, petty, animalistic, and greedy and wants to pull you down to the depths of degradation, defeat, and disaster. This negative side often makes Pisceans drink too much, and have other habits such as excessive smoking, overeating, and sexual indulgences that affect their health and mental stability.

Your chief weakness is letting other people influence you. They burden you with their problems and worries; they borrow money from you and never pay it back; they involve you in love affairs that end disastrously. Your karma is usually very severe when you give in to this basic, low side of your nature.

You must strive to rise to the true spiritual destiny that is promised by your ruling planet Neptune. This beautiful planet is high and lofty, idealistic and spiritual, and when you reflect its peace, beauty, and love, you can become illumined and achieve the ultimate destiny of greatness promised by your stars.

ADVICE FOR ALL SIGNS OF THE ZODIAC

Now that you know your true destiny according to the stars, let this book be your guide to fulfillment and joy. Occasionally read this book again, especially those sections pertaining to your own sign of the zodiac and those of your loved ones, family, and friends.

Try to follow the inclinations given for compatibility with various signs. Remember, no sign is better than another. Each is given an equal opportunity to work out his pattern of destiny and achieve greatness. It is true that some signs, notably Leo and Aquarius have been given more spectacular talents, but there are always pitfalls and weaknesses that cause them to be no more brilliant than the other signs of the zodiac.

If you were born in the difficult sign of Capricorn under stern Saturn's rulership, realize that this will give you a hard life, but you can win high goals through the character it builds. You will be fully compensated for the many hard experiences you will have in your life and the rewards can be great.

You may choose the upward path no matter what sign you were born in, and this will lead you to the fulfillment of the high potentials of that sign.

Your wheel of fortune is spinning in the celestial heights, and somewhere on this golden carousel, orbiting around our sun, there is an invisible tapestry of dreams, which carries your individual imprint of glory, fame, and fortune. Find that dream within your heart and soul; live up to its ideals of peace, love, beauty, and joy; share your good with others; and have faith in the invisible power back of life which guides you and directs you to your ultimate destiny of greatness and love.